Aging for Beginners

AGING

for

Beginners

EZRA BAYDA

with Elizabeth Hamilton

Wisdom Publications
199 Elm Street
Somerville, MA 02144 USA
wisdomexperience.org

Library of Congress Cataloging-in-Publication Data
Names: Bayda, Ezra, author. | Hamilton, Elizabeth, 1942–
Title: Aging for beginners / Ezra Bayda; with Elizabeth Hamilton.
Description: Somerville, MA: Wisdom Publications, 2018. |
Identifiers: LCCN 2017054467 (print) | LCCN 2017061378 (ebook) |
   ISBN 9781614295020 (ebook) | ISBN 9781614294771 (pbk.: alk. paper)
Subjects: LCSH: Aging—Religious aspects—Buddhism. | Spiritual
   life—Buddhism.
Classification: LCC BQ5435 (ebook) | LCC BQ5435 .B39 2018 (print) |
   DDC 294.3/4440846—dc23
LC record available at https://lccn.loc.gov/2017054467
ISBN 9781614294771   ebook ISBN 9781614295020

22 21 20 19   5 4 3

Cover design by Jess Morphew. Photo of authors walking on the beach by June Cressy. Set in Janson MT Pro 12.125/16.

*To all of the starving and suffering children throughout the world,
with the wish that they may someday have the opportunity
to experience the life of a contented geriatric*

Contents

Preface

MY SPIRITUAL SEARCH began when I was twenty, out of trying to make sense of my constant feeling of anxiety and confusion—a state I later came to call "the anxious quiver of being." My initial attempts, mainly reading and journaling, gave me a degree of intellectual understanding, but did little to relieve the anxiety. Then, in 1970, at age twenty-six, I started a daily meditation practice—beginning in earnest with a disciplined approach to the path of self-discovery. I was truly a beginner, with both a seriousness of purpose and an open curiosity to learn whatever I could. Now, after over forty-eight years of practice, and despite experiencing and learning a great deal, I find I am once again a beginner. Older age, and particularly the challenges of an aging body, have made it clear that there is still a lot to learn. The truth is, we're all beginners when it comes to the process of aging.

The idea of writing this book arose several years ago shortly after I developed kidney cancer and related complications—but I felt that I couldn't write it until I had more clarity. As a beginner in the process of aging I felt that I didn't have a broad enough perspective, and that my words therefore wouldn't be helpful to anyone. But when I talked to Josh Bartok, my friend and editor, he reminded me of something that I had forgotten: that just communicating about my own struggle is something that might be helpful to those dealing with their own similar struggles. So as I observed and worked with my own experiences, as frustrating as they sometimes were, and as I began to put down the words, I found that articulating my struggle forced me to clarify it—for myself, and hopefully for others. It also helped me to find some of the perspective that had previously eluded me. The experience of writing this book, especially repeatedly working through the various techniques and practices, has been invaluable to me.

Much has been written about aging in recent years—which isn't surprising, given that the percentage of people in the United States over the age of sixty-five has risen to a historical high of 15 percent. But aging doesn't begin when we're sixty-five. The experience of aging is very much based on our perception. When we're twenty, thirty may look to us like seventy. When we're forty, the thought of being sixty-five may seem as if life will be essentially over. And then, when we're sixty-five or seventy-five, we may still feel inwardly like we're in our forties. The point is, we can feel "old" at any time along our life process. When serious illness or incapacity strikes, for instance, or when we lose someone, we may understand, at least temporarily, the fact that we don't have endless time. And those with chronic pain, regardless of their age, may wake up each morning feeling the burden of having to face another day.

It's often said that the process of a human life can be described as "diapers to diapers." Another frequent quip is that "aging is not for wimps." Philip Roth put it even more emphatically when he wrote: "Old age is not a battle. It's a massacre." These three comments are humorous, sure, but also a testament to the fact that getting older can be an experience that is often difficult to navigate. This is not to say that we can't live with vigor and vitality into our sixties and seventies and perhaps beyond, and of course, we may still live happy and meaningful lives. And many articles promote a can-do attitude—putting an emphasis on staying physically fit, socially active, and engaged in everyday activities. All of these things may indeed be helpful and good—yet we also have to recognize that sometimes these things may not be possible, and even when they are, they may not be enough. Sometimes the realities of aging may present difficulties that nothing in our life has truly prepared us for.

The majority of this book will address the difficulties in aging that exercise, social contact, and meaningful activities alone cannot address. Moreover, there are times when a can-do attitude may in fact be counterproductive; fighting to change the things we cannot change is never helpful—such things as the loss of our strength and physical abilities, the loss of our friends, the objective fact that we will one day surely die. But learning to relate to these objective difficulties in a new way is both possible and meaningful.

Perhaps we can start by asking this: what makes getting older so potentially difficult? Certainly, as part of the menu of aging, there will be loss and the grief that follows it—grief not just for the loss of loved ones, but also for the loss of our youth, our health, our appearance, and our feelings of significance. For some there will be loneliness and helplessness. Often, there may be anxiety and depression, especially around the uncertainty of what the future will bring. Many feel the world is changing so fast, especially technologically, that they feel left behind. For all, there will probably be some degree of pain and an increasing sense of the finality of death.

But the menu of aging has a second page, an additional section: "Possibility." There is possibility because people are now

living longer than ever before—from ten to twenty years longer than our grandparents. Being older no longer means that
we are necessarily sick and incapacitated—or that we have to
withdraw from active pursuits. For some, old age may be a new
stage of life—*a stage of renewal*—in which our inner life can be
experienced as being of equal importance with our outer life.
This gives us the possibility of understanding what this life is
really about, including our place within it.

There's the possibility that we can understand, on the deepest level, that the gradual breaking down of the body is to be
expected as part of the natural order of things. And then, when it
happens, instead of fighting it, there's the possibility of learning
to accept it with equanimity, realizing that our new difficulties
don't mean that our life is now over. And then, in between the
periods of difficulty or pain, we may have increased appreciation for what is actually present and be better able embrace the
everyday treasures of being alive.

Although aging can certainly be difficult, it can also be a
surprisingly rewarding period of our life. Accordingly, a good
portion of this book will explore how we can use our aging to
enhance the quality of our daily living. Unfortunately, though,
there are no foolproof formulas or simple guidelines for navi-
gating the aging process. No matter what we read or learn about
how to cope with aging, the actual experience for ourselves
will much more likely be a gradual back-and-forth process of
confusion and insight.

One of the sources of suffering in aging arises if we take on the
identity of "an old person" or "a sick person"—and then start to
see our environment as a source of danger rather than fulfillment.
If we start to look at everything solely in terms of how we can
cope, our life becomes very narrow. And yet, while we certainly

don't want to fall into such a dark place, at the same time it is necessary to honestly acknowledge that we are, in fact, getting older or losing our good health or perhaps some of our abilities to cope as we once did. To meet this skillfully, we have to give up pretending that we are the same person we were when we were younger and healthier. At some point we may even realize the value of acknowledging the fact that we will die, even though we have no idea when that will be. This acknowledgment doesn't have to be morbid or a lament; in fact, with the clarity that our life will someday surely end, we may experience the sense of lightness that comes when we no longer identify so strongly with our bodies. This is a fine line we need to learn how to walk— accepting we are older or unwell, without assuming that this is *all* that we are.

As we get older and it hits us that our days are limited, we can more easily prioritize how we spend our time and energy, based on what is truly important to us. For me, there has been a definite change in my life perspective, as well as subtle changes in how I am living my life. There is less dwelling on petty worries and less willingness to let anger or fear dictate my life. I have found that I am less afraid to do the things I want to do—even and especially the ones I previously held back from doing. I am also less inclined to do things out of a sense of obligation that is no longer so important to me.

Hopefully, for all of us, in aging we can become more appreciative of many of the little delights throughout the day that we so often miss. And we certainly will want to communicate and connect more deeply with those we most care about. But perhaps one of the greatest gifts of aging is acquiring the wisdom to live as best we can from kindness and love.

PART I

Understanding the Terrain

1

The Basic Predicament

IT'S SOMETIMES SAID that aging is difficult because each day brings us closer to death—but though this certainly may play a part, the truth is, we may not even think about death all that often. Yet there are a variety of other factors that, when combined, can make this last stage of life particularly challenging. We start with the fact that we are all beginners when it comes to the process of aging—none of us has ever done any of this before. This alone can make it seem daunting as we face one challenge after another.

Even so, there is something we can do. The rest of this book will address how to approach these challenges in a way that can radically alter how we experience our aging.

The Human Factor

We all have an innate craving for safety, security, and control—this is part of how humans are wired for survival. Accordingly, it's difficult for us to accept the reality that so little of life is subject to our complete control. We may want to believe that we're in control, in the same way that the steersman thinks he's in control of his boat. A steersman moves his rudder and to some extent he can determine where his boat will go—but the stream is going at its own speed, and there may well be unknown twists and turns and rapids ahead. Like him, we may occasionally realize that we're not in control, but as soon as our boat hits the quiet waters, we fall back into the illusion that we are in charge of what happens. Because we simply don't want to feel the uncertainty and helplessness that come up when our illusions fall short, our response is often to deny, or resist, or fight the inevitable—in our search for something stable to hold on to. Of course, we will want to do the best we can with our changing circumstances, but that's different from demanding that we have control.

When we experience the difficulties around aging, one of our first reactions might be to ask *why*: we may analyze the situation by asking, *Why is this happening to me?*, *Why am I depressed?*, *Why am I so tired?*, *Why am I anxious?*—and so on. We ask why, in part, because we want certainty; we want to avoid the anxious quiver in our body, the discomfort of losing our illusions of control. Yet no matter how hard we try to maintain these illusions, aren't we all just one doctor's visit away from the sense of total helplessness? This is a crucial part of the predicament of aging.

On the surface, there's nothing wrong with trying to be safe or comfortable. What makes this area problematic is that, at an early age, our survival mode takes over and becomes one of our main motivations. Then, as we get older, we suffer the consequences of having pushed aside some of our other basic, natural urges—like curiosity, appreciation, and living from our true openhearted nature. Until we know how to cultivate these more positive urges, our lives become narrower and increasingly less satisfying, especially as we experience the loss of safety and security that comes as our bodies begin to gradually break down.

The Existential Predicament

All of us have an inborn desire for certainty, meaning, and structure. Yet, how does this square with the fact that we live in a world where impermanence is the nature of reality? We get sick, we get old, and we eventually die. Accordingly, all of our attempts to find a *permanent* ground to stand on will eventually fail. This is one of the main sources of our fundamental existential anxiety—the anxious quiver in our Being.

Yet, it's not just the fact of impermanence that causes us to have anxiety and suffer—it's our resistance to accepting impermanence as an inevitable aspect of life. The inexorability of aging pushes us to confront the clash between what we want—security and comfort—and the reality of what is. Trying to avoid the unwanted seems to be deeply ingrained in the human psyche, and if we forcefully continue our evasions, our suffering increases.

The existential predicament starts with the fact that as humans we want a sense of secure ground. Yet somewhere along the way we may come to the frightening realization that uncertainty and groundlessness cannot be avoided. We may experience this when we are hit with a personal crisis, such as a serious relationship breakup, a financial reversal, or a troubling diagnosis. It may become clear to us that what we want is a sense of certainty and meaning—yet we live in a world that may not offer either. This is one of the essential predicaments that all of us must eventually face, and particularly so as we get older.

The existential predicament continues with the fact of our basic aloneness. At bottom, this is the tension we feel that comes when we recognize our absolute isolation—the fact that we are born alone and that we will die alone. We may not recognize this very often, but it is in sharp contrast with our deep desire for connection, protection, and our wish to be part of a larger whole.

Perhaps the most daunting part of our existential predicament is the fact that we will all someday surely die. This is in direct conflict with our deeply ingrained desire to continue to live. There's no getting around this conflict—wanting to exist and knowing that someday we will no longer be. We can posit an afterlife or take comfort in the legacy of our children or our accomplishments, but, in truth, this comfort may not be enough to prevent the anxiety from seeping through. The solution, which will be addressed in later chapters, has to come from our acceptance of the fact that we will surely die, and from our ability to surrender to this as part of the natural order of things.

Entitlements

When difficulties around aging arise—and comfort and relief are not forthcoming—or we find ourselves in situations that won't improve and may worsen, there's a feeling that life is definitely out of sync. This doesn't just apply to aging: as far back as 2,500 years ago, the Buddha pointed out that everyone has to deal with the fact that life entails discomfort and disappointment. We will always have our many problems—fears about our health, concerns about financial security, relationship difficulties, anxious striving toward success and acceptance, and so on—and these problems may feel more acute the older we get.

Still, perhaps the most basic problem, as silly as it may sound to say it outright, is that there's a part of us that really believes that *we shouldn't have any problems.* Perhaps that's a significant factor in what makes our aging seem so distressing to us: we firmly believe that we *should* have what we want. We expect good health and the ability to stay youthful and physically fit. When life greets us with illness or injury, we commonly experience frustration and even betrayal. Sometimes just getting a cold will trigger our anxieties over losing control and feeling powerless. Our sense of entitlement basically says that life should go the way we want and expect it go—and even tells us that we shouldn't have to experience discomfort. Then, when discomfort inevitably comes along, we may feel that something is wrong; we might feel it's unfair, or feel sorry for ourselves, or get angry. If we persist in this sense of entitlement, it guarantees that we will eventually feel like a victim.

As an example, for several years I regularly experienced nerve pain, which sometimes seemed that it would never go away. Even after many years of meditating I would still hear (inside my own mind) the classic lament: "It's not supposed to be this way!" This was a humbling experience, to see how easily I could still get caught in a sense of entitlement. But one of the things this taught me is that we should never underestimate the depth of our feelings of entitlement.

The source of these feelings of entitlement is the ego, the small mind that is trying to control its world, trying to have life on its own terms. We all know the silent soundtrack—"If I do this, I'll feel better"—the assumption that we can make ourselves, and life, be the way we want them to be. But this can only bring disappointment. Why? Because no matter what we do, there's no way that we can guarantee a life that is free of problems.

Complacency

It is normal to get caught up in the complacency of our routines, living our life on autopilot. As we get older and get a taste of the changing and impermanent nature of things, this may shake us out of our complacency and comfort. In fact, this can be quite unsettling. Even if we're somewhat buffered from being actively unhappy, this is still the classic case of skating on thin ice. All it takes is one crack in the ice—such as a serious threat to our health or finances—and we see how little we can count on. We begin to see we've been chasing a false sense of certainty, dependent on favorable, yet temporary, external circumstances. An old Chinese proverb sums this up: "To be uncertain is to be uncomfortable, but to be certain is to be ridiculous."

Part of our problem is that our view is so myopic that we miss the bigger point. On the survival level, the point is simply to live. Beyond survival, however, the bigger point is to live as authentically as possible. Why? Because it's our nature to do so. Our true nature strives to reveal itself, just as an acorn strives to become an oak. This is why our deepest satisfaction is to become who we truly are.

However, when complacency takes charge, we usually just go from one thing to another, often only seeing what's right in front of us. We've lived most of our lives caught in this complacent state called "waking sleep," where we're lost in or identified with whatever we're doing, rather than being actually aware of who we are and what we're doing with our life—and we end up focused primarily on wanting to be comfortable or secure in some way.

We can spend a lot of our energy trying to fortify a particular self-image, such as being strong, or competent, or helpful. We spend still more time and energy following our usual strategies, such as trying to please others in order to gain approval, or trying to prove our worth, or gain control to ward off the feeling of chaos. These strategies are always based, on some level, in fear. Without a bigger view of what life is we will continue to sleepwalk through life, discontented and lacking in a sense of purposeful living. Ultimately we need to focus, *experientially*, on one of the key issues that we all face as we age—the fact that we feel disconnected from our true nature. The remainder of the book will try to make it clear what this actually means and what we need to do about it.

Specifics of Aging

We are often faced with new and specific challenges as we get older. For example, when we have a serious illness, or begin getting one symptom after another, it's very common to see ourselves as no more than a set of symptoms. In a way, we can even take on the identity of being a "sick person." When this happens, our life becomes filled with fear. Fear is powerful, and it can make our life feel very dark and narrow. The mind can obsess with fear-based questions: What will happen to my body? What will happen if my mind starts to go? We worry about being a burden, and at the same time we worry about who will take care of us when we need help. Will anyone even care?

It is also not uncommon to worry about losing what we have. This becomes even more acute as we age, particularly when we regularly experience the loss of our physical abilities and our health. It's likely that we will begin to lose our physical strength, stamina, and flexibility. For some this is the hardest thing. No longer having the same energy and vitality can easily spiral down into depression. For others, the hardest part of getting older is the seemingly endless parade of health issues. Sometimes it seems that as soon as one pain or symptom goes away, another one appears. Over time this can make us weary; at times it can seem as if our life is essentially over.

For some, a major difficulty in aging comes with the changes in our appearance; there are those painful moments when we realize we no longer look attractive or appealing and that there's no going back. When we look in the mirror, we can see the graying of our hair and the increasing wrinkles of our skin. We can feel the pains in our joints and the aches in our muscles. We can't see as well or hear as well or walk as well. All of these losses add up to the feeling that nothing is quite the same. The simple fact is, for many, it's no fun getting old. It may seem as if everything just starts to fall apart.

Sometimes growing old means loneliness or isolation. For some, it becomes a long wait for the inevitable. For others, one of the most difficult aspects of aging is the feeling that we are no longer useful—that we have lost our place as an important or productive person. Although it is natural to give up our roles and our occupation, their absence might cause us to begin to question our identity. This is particularly difficult when we no longer have others to confirm our importance, and we lose a sense of purpose. As we become less physically able, this feeling of loss can become acute. There may also be financial issues—it can be frightening to suddenly find yourself on a fixed income, while at the same time expenses just keep going up.

In our younger years, many of these problems may seem workable, since we tend to carry on as if we have endless time. As we age, it becomes a little more difficult to hold on to this illusion. But many may still remain in denial, seeing themselves somehow as exceptions, as if the biological laws of aging don't really apply to them. After all, we've spent all of our lives pretending that only other people get old. Adjusting to the reality that we're actually "them" can be difficult. When Elizabeth and I moved into a retirement community, we were the youngest people there, so when I'd look around and see people bent over or with walkers, it was easy to believe that they were "old" and I was still "me." But sometimes, when I would walk by a glass window and see my reflection, it was impossible to pretend that I didn't look *old*. And as I began to experience my share of difficulties and losses, I had to adjust to a new reality. It didn't come easily, and I had to go through the process of reflecting on my place in the world.

Each of us has to examine where and how we get in our own way. We can start with noticing our entitled belief that life should please us and go the way we want, that we should always be healthy and comfortable. We can also observe the thinking mind, with all of its laments about the past and worries about the future, with all of its blaming and judging thoughts, including those directed toward ourselves. All of this keeps us lost and without direction.

Although it's a challenge, discovering who we are and our direction is one of the rewards of the process of aging. One of the things that this requires is seeing the extent to which we identify with our body. We are normally so convinced that the body is who we are that we redouble our efforts to control it. But we're not in control of sickness, and certainly not of old age and death. When we try to control these things, it often leads to anger and then to powerlessness and hopelessness. When we resist the realities of aging, the result is always suffering—from the small everyday distress to the dark nights that can seem overwhelming.

The Dalai Lama, when asked what surprises him most, purportedly answered, "Man—because he sacrifices his health in order to make money, then he sacrifices money to recuperate his health. And then he is so anxious about the future that he does not enjoy the present; the result being that he does not live in the present or the future. He lives as if he is never going to die, and then dies having never really lived."

Underlying this is the basic predicament: that our world is constantly changing and that there is little we can do to control it or to satisfy our innate craving for safety and certainty. But even though we can't stop our aging or control the changes that are part of getting older, we can nonetheless begin to discover and integrate some essential teachings that can be of great value.

2

The Essential Teachings

AGING, especially with the difficulties that inevitably arise, can present us with an essential choice point. Finally realizing that we don't have endless time, our priorities can begin to shift, and we can begin to live in the phase of life that can best be described as the "natural monastery." During this phase we can learn to see our difficulties no longer as obstacles, but rather as part of our path toward self-discovery and inner freedom. Cultivating this attitude is crucial. In the second and third parts of this book we will present very specific ways for working with common difficulties—such as anxiety, loss, loneliness and physical pain—but understanding the overview from this chapter is a basic prerequisite to utilizing the specific approaches that come later.

Many who follow a spiritual path are familiar with Buddha's noble truths. There are many versions of these, but the essential teaching is that everything is temporary and that nothing in life can be certain. We suffer because the mind can't accept the reality of impermanence, and the more the mind resists this by searching for some permanent ground, the more we suffer. In other words, it is not just the outer circumstances of change and uncertainty that are the problem, but how we deal with them. Once we understand that it is the mind, or ego, that is an integral part of the problem, we have the opportunity to cultivate a new way of seeing and relating—a way which can reduce our suffering and bring a degree of equanimity. Using the difficulties of aging as our natural monastery, it is possible to cultivate a mind that can adapt to uncertainty and change. For example, when confronted with new and changing circumstances, instead of saying "Oh no—not this!" we can learn to greet them with the curious mind that says, "So this is what's next—let's see what it will be like."

This may not always (or ever) be easy. Our fears around aging, particularly when we increasingly experience discomfort and pain or sense the beginning of the loss of our mental faculties, can become a dark shadow that goes with us everywhere. A vague sense of doom can become a constant companion, and when that happens, we might lose our sense of appreciation and vitality. The more vulnerable we feel, the more widespread the fear becomes, and our lives may feel like they're spinning out of control.

Added to this, the way we perceive old age may increase our sense of its inherent difficulty. When we talk about old age, the words we use to describe our perceptions actually shape the way we view and react to our world—and it's often true that our culture describes these things in terms of burden and frailty, and focuses on pain or discomfort. These societal views of what old age is supposed to be tend to emphasize loss and helplessness and decline. In other words, is it possible to look at old age with different words and concepts?

Let's consider what it might mean to regard old age as the natural monastery. In a monastery, which we might enter when we're very young, we voluntarily give up control of our life situation in order to live in peace and solitude. Although we may not want to live in solitude as we age and still want to have at least some degree of control over our life, nonetheless we can devote this time to a deeper inner quest—the essence of monastery life. We can prioritize having fewer distractions, leaving more time for meditation, prayer, reading, and writing, as well as being in nature. Consequently, we can begin to look at our life in terms of the positive qualities of getting older.

When we do this, we have the possibility of focusing on this stage of life as a period of renewal, including cultivating the ability to see life more clearly, to live more from kindness and gratitude, to become less caught in our attachments, and to appreciate the innumerable delights that are always right in front of us. Many believe that children have a natural sense of wonder, which becomes dulled and lost as they age, but in actual fact children mostly take life for granted, and our sense of wonder only develops as a result of using aging as a stage of self-discovery and renewal. No longer pretending that we have endless time, nor ignoring how thin beneath us the ice actually is, we can fully appreciate the line from Camus: "Autumn is a second spring, when every leaf is a flower."

There is another useful teaching, often attributed to the Buddha, that we can use as a guiding principle: "In the end this is what matters most: How well did you love?" With this in mind, as we learn to cultivate a new way of seeing, we learn to always aim toward love. The question is: how do we do this?

Perhaps we think there is some secret formula or that we have to do something special to bring love to the fore, but the only "secret" is in learning how to see and relate to whatever our life is right now in a new way. This has to include even the things we find difficult, the things we don't want—the aching body, the limited stamina, the feeling of loss of purpose, the mind that seems to be slipping. When we can work with our own self-defeating attitudes around our difficulties, love is more likely to be available to us.

It's essential to see the power of our unexamined beliefs. Aging, for example, can seem so much more problematic if we have the view that life itself should forever follow *our* agenda. This limiting view comes from a sense of entitlement—a belief that life should always give us comfort, pleasure, and ease. Sadly, this keeps us from realizing that *the fullest and richest experience of life often comes as a result of the difficulties that life presents, where we are forced to go deeper.* In this way, disappointment can often become our greatest teacher. The crisis of facing the changes that come as we get older can be reframed; from a fresh perspective they can be seen as an opportunity for inner growth and renewal. We learn to view discomfort as a pathway to learn and open. We can come to understand that disappointment and pain can actually be tenderizers for the heart, awakening us to love.

During this process, there is a point at which an essential shift occurs in our Being. We move from being stuck in a life whose primary goals are comfort, security, approval, and control—all of which fortify self-centeredness and unhappiness—to a growing orientation toward wanting to live more from our deepest values. This shift is not like a change in mood, or a temporary phase, or even a change in attitude; it is an actual change in our way of Being. This shift deepens our willingness to persevere, and although strong emotions and old patterns may resurface once in a while, fundamentally there is no turning back from the natural monastery. Without this shift in our Being we will always be at the mercy of our moods, desires, opinions, and emotions, as well as of our ever-changing external circumstances. In other words, we will perpetuate our old ways of seeing and being, which keep us caught in a life that alternates between complacency and unhappiness.

All of us at times need to be shaken out of our complacency. It is so easy to get lost in imagined comfort, and it is equally easy to get stuck in our misery. If we are unwilling to look at our habitual mental attitudes and deeply ingrained emotional habits, it is very difficult to change them.

First we have to ask, who are we to begin with? For example, what is this "self" other than a physical body and a set of dispositions called a personality? Yet, don't we try to protect this "me" at all costs? To make the change or transformation that's possible as we age, we first have to see how seriously we take the little things, such as our upsets and our discomforts, without being serious enough about the bigger things, such as living from our deepest values. It's understandable that we're uncomfortable when we have physical symptoms, or feel lonely or unappreciated, but we're not nearly uncomfortable enough about how disconnected we are from what is most important, and how rarely we experience the love that is our nature. Remember, we're not talking about judging ourselves as lacking; rather we're looking closely at the nature and magnitude of what makes aging so difficult.

Perhaps the one thing that can point us in the right direction is truly experiencing, within ourselves, the "crisis of aging." This comes about when we experience the emotional realization that we don't have endless time—and that the amount of time we have left is uncertain. We don't have to wait until we're "old" to experience this—it can happen at any point in our lifetime. Seeing the full significance of this can be the wake-up call that we need to foster a reprioritizing toward doing what we feel is of most value. The emotional realization that we will someday surely die can certainly bring up fear and intensify that anxious quiver in our Being. But facing that very fear with compassionate awareness can be truly life-transforming. One of my favorite lines from Nietzsche comes to mind: "One must have chaos in oneself to give birth to a dancing star." And from this chaos we are moved in the right direction, which is always toward deeper clarity and greater love.

The clarity and wisdom that can come from living in the natural monastery allow us to understand more clearly who we are and where we stand in the world. We no longer have to be caught up in living out of the past, or out of old self-images. It is certainly understandable to reflect on the past, but if we get caught clinging to our personal history, our reflections can easily become an obstacle. Instead, the focus needs to be on being here in the present—exactly as we are right now. Surprisingly, this can often bring an experience of equanimity, as we discover that this life, despite its difficulties, is enough. When a difficulty arises, we're able to see the difference between a lump in our oatmeal and a lump in the breast. Since life is always unpredictable, when a cancer diagnosis does arrive, for instance, even if it temporarily throws us for a loop, we can remember that this difficulty can be worked with and that our efforts can eventually take us back to basic sanity.

It's good to remember that we will always be subject to our desires for comfort and our avoidance of pain. Although we may begin to see things clearly and no longer be at the whim of old behavior patterns, it is naive to imagine that these desires will not continue to arise at times. Deep learning seems to come gradually, with constant testing by life's ever-changing circumstances. For example, a great test for me is when life circumstances suddenly change and I feel a sense of loss of control, as happened when I received a kidney cancer diagnosis. For a brief time I succumbed to the imagined chaos, but once I saw what was going on, I was able to learn from it by seeing through my strong attachment to my body and to control. The same is true when I feel the anxiety that comes with each new symptom—reminding me that I am, in fact, getting older. At one point I believed that I needed to be able to become free from such stress. But interestingly, I've learned that I can actually view anxiety as helpful, as a wake-up to look a little deeper at what is going on, and as an opportunity to become free of whatever I may be attached to. This is what it means to see our difficulties as a path to inner growth. This changes the stress response to a healing one, by reminding us where our attention needs to go. By relating *to* the anxiety rather than *from* it, the stress is no longer dominant, and equanimity in the moment is possible.

One of the particular stresses associated with aging relates to our physical bodies. In our culture there's a great emphasis on body image, and also on long life. One of the ways that we can experience freedom as we age is through the realization that we are more than just our bodies. What does this mean? For me it means that even when the body is hurting I don't have to identify with that hurt as being all that I am. I can instead focus on a fuller experience of the moment. For example, I can feel the air as it becomes the breath; I can feel the breath as it becomes the air around me; I can feel a sense of my own Being and perhaps a larger sense of what life is, in which the painful parts can float more freely. This often results in the inward satisfaction from being more aware, more in touch with myself. This is one of the essential teachings of the natural monastery. Through a sincere meditation or prayer practice— or however we learn to experience an inner spaciousness—we can begin to see that the ego's narrow view is not the only version of reality. Once we experience this, we are more willing to face difficulties with a desire to learn and grow from the experience.

Another stress we feel as we age is associated with the inevitable periods of sadness and grief. Although these feelings are a natural part of aging, such as when losing a loved one or some ability we have taken for granted, when they occur we often think that something is wrong. In particular, as depression sets in, we may think that something is drastically wrong with us. But there's another way to view this. For example, as our self-images are stripped away and we can no longer rely on our usual psychological props, such as trying harder or being needed, we may certainly feel a loss, but in the natural monastery we discover that this may be a loss that is worth going through. Perhaps the loss will leave us open to taking in life in a new way. The depression may feel like a dark night, but by going through it we may be able to experience a new day—one that has more clarity and appreciation.

Even the loss of our physical strength and stamina, which we at first lament, can be seen differently. When we can no longer always be on the go and have to take more and more periods of rest, instead of seeing this as a sign of our decline, we have the opportunity to see it as part of the natural process—a process that now provides us with a time for increased reflection and inward awareness. This is a radical change in how we relate to our experience. Now, for me, when I'm tired, I no longer experience it as "the beginning of the end." It has become easier to welcome and embrace the time as a chance to slow down and be truly present. I've learned that living genuinely doesn't require that I *do* something; all it requires is that I learn how to just *be*.

One thing we should be wary of is the temptation to rely on easy solutions, like the idea of mind over matter. In its popular form the teaching is: if you don't mind, it doesn't matter, or the way you think about things can make them be the way you want them to be. This is much too simple. The essential teachings regarding aging are often subtle and all require a degree of effort, yet the benefit of our efforts is that they can lead to a clarification of what's most important. This gives us a sense of freedom to choose to do the things we most value and to choose not to do the things that go against the way we truly want to live. Personally, I have chosen to avoid social situations that primarily involve small talk. At the same time I have chosen more honest communication with the people I most care about. "Honest" doesn't mean telling others all of our opinions and reactions; rather, it means risking vulnerability to be revealing about what is actually going on with us. As well, we may be willing to go against our fears and take risks we wouldn't have previously taken. With an increased sense of the poignancy of life, the general movement is away from complacency and diversions to living a more authentic life.

Living authentically is not something that comes easily, since it is quite different from what seems "natural," based on the habitual way we've been living. As much as anything it requires a clear perspective. When aging presents us with difficulties, and at the same time the outside world seems to be out of kilter, it's very easy to get caught up in believing how bad things may seem in our country. The outer situations and our emotional reactions to them seem to intensify each other. But it's helpful to have some knowledge of history to be able to see our current times in clear perspective. There have been many periods, in every country, where things have been drastically worse than they are right now. Just a few examples include wars, famine, natural disasters, genocide, and devastating epidemics like the plague and influenza. When we can see our present times within this kind of historical perspective, it's possible that the world won't seem quite as grim—and as a consequence, our own personal difficulties may not seem so exaggerated.

Even if we have a broad overview of what's going on, it's still easy to get lost in shortsighted "goals." We might have the goal of "trying to be happy," and not realize that, as we age, happiness doesn't come from making it a goal. Genuine happiness, as we get older, comes from being able to appreciate the ride, being curious about and embracing what our life is, rather than trying to get somewhere or trying to feel a particular way.

We also need to be alert to, and decline, the tendency to fight the signs of aging, since they aren't going anywhere. This doesn't mean we don't try to take care of ourselves. Yet, inevitably, there are things that we cannot change. Striving constantly to overcome them, in the hopes that doing so will make us happy, guarantees added stress. The solution is to begin to see that *whatever* is on our plate is our opportunity to become inwardly free, which in turn guides us toward a deeper and more genuine equanimity. As French author Marcel Proust put it: "The real voyage of discovery consists not in seeking new landscapes but in seeing with new eyes."

There's a heartening shift that occurs as we learn to be honestly present with our life, just as it is. This makes it possible to move from our narrow, self-centered preoccupations to a more life-centered awareness. Paradoxically, bringing attention to whatever arises in the moment—including our pretenses, our protections, our unquestioned beliefs, and our fears—allows us to see that these self-imposed boundaries are not fixed realities.

As we bring awareness to the many layers of our conditioning and the struggles that arise as a result of that conditioning, the power of that conditioning slowly diminishes. This enables us to live life more from our natural Being and a vaster sense of what life is. We can realize, experientially, that the words *connectedness* and *love* are more than just words; they are the direct experience of embracing aging as our path toward self-discovery. When we're truly present to this reality, we can appreciate the sweetness of the moment, even when the moment isn't conventionally sweet. As the heaviness of old beliefs about life falls away, there's a lightness of being and at times a wonderful taste of inner freedom.

3

Intention and Aspiration

WHEN WE START on the spiritual path of self-discovery, our intention, our aspiration to live more genuinely, may only be about 5 percent of our various motivations. The other 95 percent may be on the usual things—security, comfort, looking good, pleasure, and so on. During this phase we may dabble in spiritual practice. We may meditate on and off, go to groups, and maybe even attend retreats. But there may still be very little commitment to truly living in a new way.

Over time our aspiration may grow—especially as we get older and become increasingly disappointed in the failure of our usual life strategies, such as trying to please, trying to hide, trying to win. We see that these strategies do very little in truly bringing peace of mind. At some point, we may realize how painful it is to continue pursuing these strategies, which keep us caught in a life that fluctuates between complacency and unease. We need to ask: What is required to kindle our aspiration toward self-discovery? What turns the key, so that we can begin to view aging as a stage of renewal—a way to live in the natural monastery of life?

The real tipping point comes when our aspiration goes from 49 to 51 percent. This is the point where the teeter-totter of on-again, off-again spiritual efforts finally settles into a more stable and constant place. Although we're bound to alternate through phases of spiritual enthusiasm and spiritual dryness, our aspiration can still continue to become more and more the central orientation of our lives.

It's good to consider where we are on this teeter-totter—to reflect on how serious our intention is to live more authentically. As we get older, we have an opportunity to cultivate our aspiration actively. Even though aspiration seems to be in part something we are born with, there are still two primary ways that we can feed it: one is with our *intention*, and the other is with our *attention*. The interplay of intention and attention goes to the heart of what it means to live in a truly authentic way.

Intention is crucial. Gurdjieff, a spiritual teacher known for his deep psychological insight, once said that without intention we will continue to sleepwalk through life on automatic pilot. Intention helps us keep the point in mind, highlighting the direction in which we aspire to go. In each activity we can ask ourselves: Do I intend to be more present? To refrain from judging and blaming? To experience gratitude? To live from kindness?

Intention can be a strong motivator, since it arises from, as well as feeds, our aspiration to live with more presence. In the beginning our intention may be small and even somewhat self-centered. It may be about striving to get something, to get somewhere, or to feel a particular way, like forever youthful and full of energy. These are actually ego-driven strategies, not the call of genuine aspiration. Fortunately for us, they always lead to disappointment, and paradoxically, this disappointment can remind us to connect more with our genuine aspiration and intention.

I remember an interesting conversation with one of my teachers. While talking to her, I mentioned that I had been doing a kindness meditation and found it really helpful. She asked me what I was trying to do with it, what my intention was, and I couldn't answer in the moment—but when I reflected on it, I realized that I was trying to artificially change my feelings, to feel some other way than I was feeling. After I reflected on it, I changed the words to the meditation to align them more with my aspiration to learn to be with my life as it is, rather than as something that sounded nice, but was actually an artificial way to try to feel kind. A kindness meditation that I've found genuinely helpful is included later in the book.

The point is that we need to be aware of our intention in order to see clearly where we want to go, and also to see the path that leads in that direction. At first our intention may be somewhat unconscious, as in my case with the kindness meditation. Part of learning to live more wakefully is to make this intention conscious, and this can be helped by making a *statement of intention*. Such a statement can be fairly straightforward: "I aspire to live with as much presence as possible," or "May I live from the open heart."

As we mature, our intention needs to be based on a reprioritizing of what is most important to us. I have three vows that I say first thing in the morning before I meditate, as an expression of my highest aspiration:

May I say Yes to everything—going to the root of my fears.
May I be aware without ceasing—letting life just be.
May I see the face of God in everyone—dwelling in the
    heart of awareness.

Regarding "the face of God": I'm using the word *God* here not referring to any specific religion, but as a way of referring to a sense of connectedness, the ineffable energy that unites all and everything. These kinds of vows may sound idealistic, but

I don't say them with the expectation that they'll be met. Instead, they help me remember my intention for the day. Here we have to be watchful not to turn our intention into goals that we try to meet, as they can then be misused as one more way to judge ourselves as inadequate. I see these words as pointers to what is closest to our heart, so even if they sound lofty, a quote from Thomas Merton may help put them in the proper perspective: "Of what avail is it if we can travel to the moon if we cannot cross the abyss that separates us from ourselves? This is the most important of all journeys and without it, all the rest are useless."

It's critical to understand that this kind of intention is not something we arrive at through logic and reasoning. It is more of an existential choice that arises from our experience in living. For example, seeing our difficulties as part of the path of self-discovery, rather than as obstacles on the path, is not necessarily a logical position. Instead, it is a viewpoint that we adopt because of its experiential impact on our life; it reminds us to bring attention to our everyday difficulties—like worrying about our loss of energy and stamina or concern about our changing appearance. Then, these challenges can be used to free ourselves from excessive attachment to the body or our vanities. It is helpful to remember our intention before we start our day, before we meditate, and before each new activity, like going to a meeting, or a doctor's appointment, or even on a vacation. But the point isn't to make ourselves feel guilty, or go overboard and take ourselves and our every move too seriously; it's simply a reminder to take our priorities to heart.

Intention is simply a guide. Without it, as Gurdjieff said, we'll often go into our habitual pattern of sleepwalking through life. I read of one teacher who tried to cultivate a "GPS mind"—a mind that would help one's life stay on course, and help one to know where it was going off on a detour. With a clear intention we can make the choices that best serve our highest values. When we make our inevitable detours, our GPS mind can remind us to pause and look at what we're doing. It can also remind us what we need to do to get back on course—perhaps something as simple as taking a few deep breaths.

And yet, although intention is crucial, it is not enough by itself. As you may have already discovered, it's not possible to be more present just because we *want* to be. It's essential to commit to making the efforts necessary to bring our intention to fruition. This requires our efforts of attention, or bringing awareness to present moment experience, which is the primary tool for making our intention a living reality. Awareness practice can vary greatly; it can be narrow and focused, such as in meditation where we bring a concentrated attention to the breath. Or it can be more open, as in paying attention to whatever arises. It can also be focused on qualities like kindness or gratitude.

It's important to understand that simply paying attention does not necessarily mean that we're living more awake. Paying attention becomes part of our spiritual practice only when it is about what we consider to be most important. When I was a carpenter, I paid meticulous attention when I ran a circular saw, or worked high up on buildings. But this was attention in the narrowest sense, like focusing on a task or a sport. As valuable as this is—it can keep us alive or uninjured after all—it is mere concentration, and it often lacks the intention to live more awake or free from attachment to a particular outcome. The degree to which we are willing to pay attention as part of our intention to live more from our deepest values reflects the depth of our resolve to awaken, to live genuinely, and to live from kindness and love.

We may think we're serious about our spiritual life, but at some point it may become obvious to us that the majority of the time, even during prayer or meditation, we choose to let our attention continue to wander—to plans, worry, conversations, meaningless daydreams—without making the effort to return to presence. We do this even though we may have heard over and over the teachings about the need to persevere in being present to what the moment holds. Yet, how often do we remember to pay attention in this way? We may remember to feel the occasional breath or to notice a thought. But the determination to bring continuous attention to what is actually going on has to be cultivated again and again. And when we become aware of our gaps in attention—we also need to remember not to judge ourselves, but rather notice where we got caught, and then simply return to being attentive.

This may sound like an ideal or impossible task, but truthfully, to be serious about our path, rather than just dabbling, requires that we be prepared to pay the price of giving up our various self-centered attachments—to our opinions, addictive patterns, our blaming, our moods. We also have to give up the self-deceptions that we cling to for comfort: the illusion that we are in control, that we are special, or that we are a separate self, independent of everything around us. But perhaps we first have to give up the illusion that we have endless time.

The realization that we don't actually have limitless time helps us become more willing to reprioritize our values. At this point, we're more able to commit to being present as often as possible, and to remaining present for as long as possible. Even though at times the process of aging can leave us feeling weary or discouraged, being present is what leads to a greater experience of our own Being—a deep equanimity that we will never experience by just following the ego's desires, or by avoiding what we find unpleasant.

To summarize: We start with the intention to awaken, to live more genuinely. With a soft effort, we refine and expand that intention over time, becoming more and more clear about where we're going and what it takes to get there. We then begin to pay attention to what is—to what is actually present right now—at first perhaps minimally, haltingly, and with much resistance. The ego-self resists any attempts to shine light on its fictional world of beliefs, self-images, and self-perpetuating fears. The interesting paradox is that we lose our identification with our "self" by paying meticulous attention to the arising of self in all its manifestations. Then, at some point, an inner change occurs: the 49 percent tips into the 51 percent, and our aspiration not to waste time becomes increasingly the propelling force in our life. This is a turning point in truly giving up the illusion that we have endless time.

But this does not happen easily or without effort. Ultimately the effort to cultivate our intention and commit to the seriousness of the task—of being present and paying attention with precision and perseverance—is what allows us to live the genuine life of presence and awakening.

This is what allows us to gradually open into clarity and love, which are the fruits of making aging our spiritual path.

Expectation and Aspiration

One of the main places we can easily get confused is in not differentiating between our *aspirations* and our *expectations*. While expectation is based in the mind, aspiration is based more in the heart, or in our essential nature. One way of understanding aspiration is to see it as our true nature striving to reveal itself. Just as an acorn becomes an oak tree, aspiration can be seen as the inherent movement right now toward the fullness of who we are. Expectation is experienced very differently, primarily because it is often characterized by ambition, neediness, and fear. The effort of aspiration is softer, not as driven by results as by the inner impulse to live more genuinely.

Everyone has expectations, including expectations of what they'll get out of pursuing a spiritual path. Often these expectations center on the hope of becoming peaceful and calm. The expectation that drove me for many years was the hope of becoming free from my anxiety and fears. After all, if meditation practice couldn't do that, what would be the point? It might be very worthwhile to reflect for a moment on what your expectations are in relation to getting older. Is the expectation that things will continue just as they are? Or perhaps that you won't really have to go through sickness, or even "old age," or death?

Having expectations is, of course, human—and not necessarily problematic, as long as we eventually see them for what they are. What becomes problematic is when our expectations are more like demands or requirements, rather than simply preferences. When we demand, or require, that life, or people, be a particular way, it will very often lead to suffering. For example, we may have the expectation that our bodies will remain somewhat healthy, but if it's a demand, it will have a much stronger emotional flavor. Gradually recognizing and working with our various requirements and demands is an integral part of the spiritual path of aging.

And yet, sometimes it's difficult to tell what exactly is driving us. Perhaps it's our aspiration to be free, but it may also be just another way of trying to fulfill our expectation that we can rid ourselves of our difficulties and consequently allow ourselves to feel better. More often what drives us is a combination of the two, as they are so easily intertwined. The main clue is that being driven by expectations will almost always be accompanied by physical tension, and a sense of *drivenness*, and will eventually lead to disappointment—primarily because they are not based on what life is, but on what we want life to be.

It's important to recognize where we're caught in our expectations or in being entitled to have life be some particular way. Think about your expectations in sitting reading this book. To find out what they are, right now ask yourself: How is this experience supposed to be? Do you expect to be entertained (unlikely!)? Informed? Inspired? Are you supposed to find the one magic key to getting older without too much anxiety, too much grief, too much difficulty?

Each one of these expectations (and myriad others) is a setup for possible disappointment—but because we know this, each time we experience disappointment it can be a reminder to look a little deeper, to see where we're caught in an expectation. And then what? We simply pause and stay present with what's there—the emotions, the bodily sensations, the frustration. The only place that we can go deeper in our self-discovery is in being present with whatever is on our plate. This is also the place where we can experience equanimity—*equanimity meaning being present with exactly what we are experiencing right now, without judgment.* This can include our disappointment, anxiety, depression, or whatever else may be present. Feeling equanimity doesn't mean these things are gone—rather it means we are present with them without judging them as bad or needing them to go away. Even though this may seem like an impossible dream, it is nonetheless the exact path to what we wish, most deeply, for our lives.

When I'm sitting in meditation, it occasionally hits me that what I most deeply want—what I have wanted ever since I began the path of meditation decades ago—is to simply dwell in the heart of awareness, and to live from that place. More than anything, this includes living from kindness, gratitude, and love. To me, this is what it means to live from aspiration, to live most authentically. It's not about getting somewhere or becoming someone else—it's about becoming who we most truly are. A big part of my own path in getting older, and in trying to live from the natural monastery of life, is to deepen this aspiration and let it be my guiding impulse.

Unfortunately, when expectations become dominant, our aspiration tends to get dwarfed. Remember, the small mind of the ego wants what it wants, often based in the desire for comfort and security, and it speaks more loudly than the softer voice of aspiration—that still, small voice that yearns to be heard. But, over time, particularly as we learn to be more inwardly quiet and open (in the ways we'll be exploring later in this book), we can hear the more deeply compelling message of our aspiration. An important part of the spiritual path is to continually feed the part of us that wants to live more awake. Whether it's through meditation, going to retreats, prayer, reading, being in nature, doing the things that touch us most deeply—we have to use whatever we can to nourish the aspiration that urges us to realize what our life really is, at the deepest, most satisfying level.

There may be times, such as a sudden change in our life or being hit with a serious illness, when we are forced to look deeply at our aspiration and intention. In these circumstances we may understand with certainty that we don't have the time to continue living on autopilot. We may want to really consider what we want the rest of our life to be. We may realize that there are certain things that we don't want to leave undone; we may want to communicate honestly with the people we really care about; we may want to drop any activities that we just do because we think we're supposed to. We may also realize that we want to spend more time in prayer or meditation or, if we're able, in nature. All of this requires a clear intention and commitment.

For real transformation to take place we may need to stay disciplined in a particular direction for however much time we have left. It's true that working with difficulties is hard, yet, as we discover, not working with them is even harder. Regardless of whether we are struggling, and regardless of conditions, it's important to keep remembering our original aspiration. Sometimes our aspiration will weaken; at times we may even lose sight of it. However, true courage requires us to continually reconstruct our aspiration and renew it in the heart. Without this kind of perseverance it is very unlikely that we will overcome the unrelenting patterns of the small mind—the very things that cause us so much of our suffering. Nietzsche spoke to this in this passage from *Thus Spake Zarathustra*: "Today your courage and your hopes are still whole. But [. . .] the time will come when that which seems high to you will no longer be in sight, and that which seems low will be all-too-near. [. . .] And you will cry, 'All is false!' There are feelings which want to kill the lonely; and if they do not succeed, well, then they themselves must die."

For me, in the last several years since my kidney cancer surgery, life has been somewhat of a roller coaster ride. I noticed myself repeatedly getting caught in my expectation that I could be in control, followed by the consequent disappointment when it became increasingly obvious that I could control hardly anything. This helped me remember my aspiration to use each of the many disappointments as my path to awakening. Sometimes, when physical discomfort is intense, or seemingly unending, it is extremely difficult to drop the expectation that things will—or should—soon get better. But certainly some of the time, when things are hard but not overwhelming, I can remember to say "Hello" to the pain, to greet it as a familiar traveling companion—an expression of a lighthearted friendliness that no longer sees the pain as the enemy.

This is an act of aspiration, and in many instances it has led to a degree of equanimity. But, there were also instances where it didn't bring equanimity, and that's the real test of the depth of our aspiration. When life is simply hard—objectively hard—with little relief even with our best efforts, it can be tempting to slip into the small mind of doubt and become discouraged. The dark winds will at times blow through all of us. The chronic or intense illness that often at some point accompanies aging can test even the strongest person's fortitude. Perhaps you've already experienced how the objective magnitude of uncertainty and groundlessness can make you just want to give up.

Yet consider the possibility that we can persevere anyway, knowing that we have little control, but nonetheless being willing to take the ride. This is a very interesting place on the path, and as I've discovered, at times there may be very little clarity. But I've also discovered that it's almost always possible to return to the breath and say "Hello" to whatever is on our plate—regardless of where it leads.

4

Meditation and Deep Relaxation

ONE OF THE GREAT BENEFITS OF AGING is being able to experience the deep satisfaction of occupying a space without an agenda—to enjoy the inner equanimity of just Being, regardless of how or where we find ourselves. But how can we come to this satisfying state? Perhaps, more than anything, the practice of meditation can help us in our aspiration to experience this inner equanimity.

There are many different ways to meditate. Since the explosion of mindfulness practice in the last decade, many equate mindfulness with meditation. However, there are hundreds of meditation centers throughout the country, teaching a variety of methods of meditation. What's important to understand is that different aspects of meditation are more useful depending on our stage of life. For example, as we get older, it is unlikely we will want to try to sit cross-legged for hours, which the young and agile can do with some ease. Nor should we expect meditation alone to be the key to good health. While meditation can be very helpful, we can't expect it to take away the inexorable aging of the body. Certainly some kinds of meditation can help lower the blood pressure and relieve stress, but so can many other things, such as gentle yoga, tai chi, and even listening to soft music.

To help clarify the practice of meditation there are two particular capacities we'll explore: deep relaxation and the quality of presence. Both are important. Deep relaxation makes it more possible to enter into a state of inner stillness. The quality of presence is the ability to truly be here, with the sense of being at home with oneself. As we age, this is particularly important, because often we will find ourselves in circumstances that are not comfortable, either physically or emotionally. So to be able to feel at home wherever we are is a great gift.

In order to experience this gift we have to be willing to put in the work. What is the work? It's a commitment to sitting in meditation on a daily basis, or at least several times a week. This doesn't have to be grueling or painful. You can sit in a chair or if necessary lie down. You can sit for just twenty minutes a day to start. However, in order to experience the fruits of meditation, you'd want to increase the time spent in meditation as you are able. And here's the real kicker: you will need to sit close to daily for the rest of your life! This may sound daunting, unless we realize that meditation is like eating, where it's obvious that the benefits depend on doing it regularly. The good news is that once you establish a meditation practice and feel its benefits, you will *want* to include that as one of your high priorities.

One of the challenges with engaging in a meditation practice, even for established meditators, is that the stresses in our lives can seem to get in the way of meditating. When troubled, the mind can be very busy, and we may never feel like we really settle down. Yet, a satisfying ongoing meditation practice requires that we be able to settle down in body and mind, regardless of what is going on. One solution is to first establish a deep relaxation practice, which involves slowing and deepening the breath. In a way this is a meditation practice in itself; as the body relaxes, the mind will eventually become more still.

Deep Relaxation

Deep relaxation is based on a breathing technique that can trigger the body's natural ability to calm down. Here is a little background: The autonomic nervous system is divided into two branches—the sympathetic and the parasympathetic. The sympathetic branch is associated with high levels of anxiety, rapid heartbeat, shakiness, panic, and other such things. The parasympathetic branch is associated with calm and a lower heart rate. The two branches cannot dominate at the same time, so the practice is to cultivate the parasympathetic response of calm and learn to be able to activate it and override the sympathetic response of panic.

With some practice, when you take slow, steady breaths, your brain gets the message that all is well and activates the parasympathetic response, which slows heart rate and digestion and promotes feelings of calm.

For deep relaxation breaths you inhale slowly through the nose and exhale quietly and slowly through the mouth. The main focus is on breathing more slowly and more deeply than normal, without forcing it. It can help to keep time by shooting for six breaths per minute, or roughly five seconds for each inhale and each exhale. It's important to work up to this practice slowly, starting with inhaling and exhaling roughly every three seconds and working your way up to every five seconds. If it feels uncomfortable to breathe that slowly, it's okay to start to breathe at whatever rate feels more relaxed. But remember, it's the slower deeper breathing that triggers the parasympathetic nervous system response of calm.

Deep Relaxation Meditation Instructions

I learned a version of this meditation from Jeanette Perkins, a hypnotherapist and long-term meditator. I began using it several years ago to prepare for kidney cancer surgery, and I found it so helpful that I've been doing it daily ever since.

Try the following deep breathing meditation once a day for two to three weeks in order to cultivate the ability to activate the parasympathetic response of calm.

To start, call to mind someone or something you love, in order to set the tone with a positive and open state of mind.

With eyes closed, take five deep breaths through the nose and exhale slowly through the mouth while you silently say "Relax." As you breathe out, imagine you can feel the tension drain out of you. Let the body relax.

Next, begin counting breaths backward from fifty to one, breathing deeply. Count on the exhale only.

The breathing should gradually be slowed to about six full breaths per minute or five seconds for each inhale and each exhale.

Feel the breath enter through the nose. Feel it in the chest. Then feel it in the abdomen area, letting it gently massage the belly on both in-breath and out-breath.

When thoughts arise, try to put them on "call waiting," and come back to maintaining a focused awareness on the breath in the body.

What does it actually feel like to breathe?

Feel the enjoyment of breathing in deeply. Feel the relaxation when breathing out.

If you lose track of the numbers, come back to the last number you remember.

When you've finished counting from fifty to one, silently repeat the following statement five times to solidify the association between the deep breathing and the parasympathetic response of calm: "When I count back from fifty, I feel calm, relaxed, and present."

To end, acknowledge and feel the calm and relaxed state in the body.

You probably need to do this meditation daily for two to three weeks in order to cultivate the ability to automatically trigger the parasympathetic response of calm. Once this meditation is established, whenever you feel anxiety or tension arise, start breathing slowly and deeply while counting backward from fifty. After a while, the level of anxiety will most likely start to drop, because, by association, you are activating the parasympathetic response of calm. This makes deep relaxation breathing a very useful tool to use anytime, anywhere. It is also an excellent meditation in itself, promoting an inwardly settled state.

Meditation

Once you've cultivated the ability to relax, it's much easier to learn and practice awareness meditation. Although there are many different ways to meditate, there are certain essentials that serve as the foundation for any genuine meditation practice. As we sit in meditation, it is crucial that our intention is to be still and silent. It's possible that we'll feel relaxed and calm as the body and mind settle down, and it's possible that at times we will not feel relaxed and calm. Accordingly, what's important is to be *aware*—to cultivate the capacity to be present to whatever comes up. The point is to pay full attention to the ever-changing states of the body and mind. This is one of the biggest challenges we face in meditation—learning to abide with awareness, no matter what comes along. This takes a lot of determination, yet aren't most of the things we find beneficial often challenging at first? However, even though it's difficult, the innate capacity to reside in what's present is nonetheless always available to us. It just takes some training, especially when what comes along isn't what we hoped for.

When we were young and healthy, we may have had ample distractions to avoid having to abide in the unpleasant. However, unaddressed, this habit leads to increasing unhappiness as we age, since we will most likely be faced with increasing discomfort and loss, including the inability to engage in many things we formerly found enjoyable or used for distraction. Let's be honest: inviting whatever shows up to come in and be here on our meditation seat is probably not what we had in mind in taking up meditation! We may have hoped to be able to start in grad school, without going through the rudiments first.

So we begin with the quiet yet active process of engaging in observation, with stillness and silence. People may imagine that inner silence means that there's no thinking going on. Actually the silence we find in meditation is the fruition of simply staying present, rather than trying to get rid of thoughts. *Meditative silence* means experiencing the moment exactly as it is, mental chatter and all.

We may discover that the beginning stages of meditation can be a series of shocks, as we realize the extent of our judgments, resistance, and boredom. Our mind can seem to be the inner equivalent of a gerbil spinning on a wheel in a cage; yet meditation invites us to get interested in all this, watching it with curiosity, rather than analyzing or judging. Even when the mind is caught in a spin cycle, we can *experience*, physically, what's going on in the body. When we're calm—we feel it in the body. If we're agitated—we feel it in the body. If the mind is busy, we observe what thoughts are present. This is empowering in a genuine way; there's something about being still and being present that's inherently satisfying.

A helpful attitude to cultivate is to see the thoughts and feelings that come up in meditation as our teachers. We can use them to learn about ourselves, rather than going into a civil war with them. Trying to fight against or change our thoughts or experience takes a huge amount of energy, and we can end up believing that we're somehow flunking meditation.

If we have a belief like this, it's important to recognize that this negative judgment is a result of what we're adding to the simple basic activity of meditation. For example, we may experience dissatisfaction if we have the expectation that through meditation we should become clear, calm, spiritual, or together, and the faster, the better. We just have to acknowledge these expectations as something that we're adding to the process— even if that doesn't immediately make them go away. The same is true of our judgments of all the things that we've regarded as faults. We can begin to see them as just part of the current inner scenery, and this awareness allows our many layers of ideals and imagined shortcomings to deconstruct.

One thing meditation may help us discover, after living many years with a somewhat simplistic view of who we are, is that our seemingly solid self is actually an amalgam of many selves rather than an unchanging single one. In a way it's almost like a television set's channels: the drama channel, the entertainment-and-escape channels, the history (or memory lane) channel, and the future planning channel—all of which cause us to lose sight of what's actually going on in the moment. One thing we can begin to do, as we watch these many selves take the stage, is to observe the struggle and striving that's involved in our often conflicting inner motives. This includes trying to prove ourselves by maintaining a self-image that we may no longer even believe in—like the belief that were supposed to appear athletic and strong, even though our body may no longer allow this. This can result in a conflict between the "me" we remember and are attached to, and the "me" that is our current reality, the one showing up right now. Sitting with this conflict in meditation, we can observe the mind going back and forth between these, along with the corresponding agitation in the body.

The important thing is to learn to be with all this, without judging it or trying to fix it. This process isn't about trying to change our behaviors; rather it's about learning to extend compassion to ourselves *just as we are right now.* Ironically, our attempts to change ourselves often keep us stuck in unhappiness. One of meditation's main maxims is *"awareness heals,"* so the solution is to observe the many habits and self-images we hold on to, and feel how these are manifested in the body. Even if genuine compassion seems elusive at first, it starts with refraining from constantly judging ourselves and others.

One of the surprising gifts of ceasing the struggle for self-improvement is that an inner spaciousness can begin to emerge, a sense of being at home in our bodies and minds. Feeling at home with ourselves may not come easily, especially if our life's pattern has been to be busy and on the go. Getting older can present a particular difficulty, since having less energy, or finding ourselves recovering from a new knee or hip, we may feel very agitated when we have to slow down. This agitation may seem even more pronounced as we sit in the stillness of meditation, with no distractions. At first this can seem anything but still, yet meditation affords us the opportunity to sit with the inner unease, and this in turn can help build *distress tolerance*, which makes being present to challenges more workable. As intense as our discomfort may be at times, simply staying physically still helps the antsiness slowly settle down, as we realize that we don't have to be constantly moving or being busy. This can free us from a great burden, and as we enter back into daily life from our meditation, we might experience a lightness and ease that feels like a breath of fresh air.

It's important to remember that meditation practice is often like a winding mountain road, with ups and downs and unexpected curves. Just when things seem more stable and settled, the tapestry interweaves with discouragement or the belief that we're failing. Through all of these ups and downs, the practice is simply to rest your mind in the breath, to feel it fully. Once you can experience the breath, rest your mind in the environment—feeling the air, hearing the sounds, sensing the spaciousness of the room. Then let awareness of the breath and the environment be experienced together, as inner and outer holding spaces in the present moment, for whatever life presents.

Recently one of my meditation students experienced a very unexpected curve on her life path. After not feeling well for a short time she was told she had extensive cancer and just a few weeks to live. After the initial shock, she turned to her meditation seat to try to find some balance. Because it was very clear that she no longer had endless time, she began to see her lifelong struggle to measure up and get approval from a whole new perspective. At this point she no longer had the energy to struggle to present herself in a favorable way, and she understood how much energy she had wasted during her life by struggling to maintain her self-image and avoid any kind of disapproval.

Although she was very weak, she was able to stay present with the breath and with this clear insight. She spoke to me about how easy it is to lose sight of what's most important and instead focus on trying to live according to the expectations of others. She knew she couldn't do her life over, but at least for her last few weeks she was able to live free from the fear of not measuring up. She was able to take in the tremendous influx of love from her family and friends and extend her own love in return. She mentioned to me that without the spaciousness of meditation she might never have come to appreciate how good her life truly was.

As we become increasingly able to remain aware of the breath and the environment, these dual anchors provide a strengthening sense of presence, both in formal meditation and in our daily activities. These two anchors have plenty of room for whatever arises—our obsessive planning, daydreams, internal conversations, and physical and emotional discomfort. Again, it helps to remember that still and silent sitting awakens our deep sense of what's most important, most real. Our awareness anchors—breath and environment—become a portal into reality, or the mystery of Being that we share with one and all. Entering into this mystery, this silence, is best served by maintaining a quiet, abiding presence in each moment. As we allow ourselves to *just be*, as difficult as it seems at first, we can contact a sense of peace that has previously seemed elusive. This requires realizing that our overactive minds—our thoughts and stories—aren't who we really are; they're part of the passing show of life, like clouds in the sky.

The dynamic at the heart of meditation practice involves simply *being* rather than doing. Our inclination turns toward openness rather than trying to fix or control or struggle. When we sit down to meditate, often the mind is very busy—and our first reaction is usually to think that this means something is wrong. This can quickly turn into self-judgment—the belief that something is wrong with *us*. We automatically think that we have to *do* something about it, and as a consequence, we habitually move into the fix-it mode.

But there's an alternative to this habitual mode. No matter what arises during meditation, no matter how we may be feeling—physically or emotionally—the practice is to simply stay still, to acknowledge what's going on, and then let it be. We don't need to "let it go"—we simply let it *be* there. Attempting to "let go" of things can actually be counterproductive: it is often code for trying to get rid of what we don't like. This is understandable, yet it's also misery-provoking.

Letting be, on the other hand, is what it means to simply be present to what is. Of course we still need active discipline to stay present, to remain still, and to be precise in observing thoughts and reactions. This in turn awakens humility and even a sense of humor as we discover our repetitive dramas and habits. We can recognize them as just old conditioning, rather than patterns that are fixed for life. Over time, indulging in them starts to become optional.

"Cheerful Perseverance Is Key to Success"

We also need to remind ourselves again and again that as straightforward as the practice of meditation may be, it can often seem very difficult. This is a byproduct of the mind's seeming unwillingness to simply let things be. This is why meditation takes a lot of perseverance. In fact, perseverance is one of the most important qualities of meditation. It helps us weather the ups and downs in times of doubt, confusion, and wondering what in the world made us want to take up meditation in the first place.

I learned about the quality of perseverance in a very unexpected way. When I was in my mid-twenties, I was very unhappy with my work as a computer programmer, and distraught about what occupation I would find suitable. Then one weekend I helped some people remodeling a barn, and although I didn't know anything about carpentry, I had an epiphany that I wanted to be a carpenter. Given my background, this realization was quite far-fetched; I not only didn't have any carpentry skills, I was also very slight (I think I weighed around 120 pounds at the time).

Someone had just given me the *I-Ching*, a book of Chinese wisdom sometimes used for guidance, and I asked it the question, "What will it take to become a carpenter?" And the answer was: "Cheerful perseverance is the key to success." Who knows why, but I actually took the phrase to heart and began looking for a job as a carpenter.

I drove from job site to job site in San Francisco and got rejected by everybody. But buoyed by the phrase, I finally got a job, and I worked for the same company for two years. During that time I faced many situations that were very difficult for me, both physically and psychologically, like trying to push a wheelbarrow full of concrete and being humiliated that I couldn't even budge it, or being told to climb up a thirty-foot ladder to fix a broken support in the ceiling. A thirty-foot ladder is really high—and I'm afraid of heights. My hands were shaking so hard I couldn't even hold a nail, so they made me come down. But I continued to rely on the phrase "cheerful perseverance is the key to success." And the phrase helped me get through the many difficulties in the apprenticeship training—including repeated experiences of humiliation.

I began a meditation practice shortly after becoming a carpenter, and the phrase about cheerful perseverance helped me immensely in learning the art and practice of meditation. The phase is not like a fortune cookie; in a way, you could say that this phrase goes to the heart of living wisely—but its meaning is somewhat subtle. What does *cheerful* mean? It's not about having a smiling face or some artificial equanimity. It's more about a willingness and a welcoming disposition. When a difficulty arises in meditation, instead of thinking something is wrong or that we need to find a solution, we see it with a kind of lighthearted curiosity. So instead of "Oh no" to whatever is arising, it's more like, "Hello—What can I learn here?" There's a willingness to enter into and work with whatever is arising.

Practicing with cheerful perseverance may require dropping our stories or self-images; for example, when I encountered my very busy mind in meditation, I had to drop my familiar story of "This is too hard; I can't do it." Of course you can't drop something before you're aware of what it is—whether it's our beliefs or our emotions. Part of the value of meditation is being able to clearly see what we're believing and feeling, thus allowing us to drop them. Time and again I had to drop my indulgence in particular emotions, like confusion or anxiety.

What does perseverance mean? *To persevere* literally means to be steadfast. Perseverance makes it possible to stay with what life presents, through all of the difficulties, the valleys, the dry spots—where we forget what we've learned and even doubt the value of meditation. Perseverance is what makes it possible to sit in meditation through discomfort, to sit when we don't feel like it, to sit when we're bored or tired. It's easy to turn perseverance into what has been referred to as a "slimy virtue"—where we do our duty in a martyred way or to make ourselves feel special. That's why I describe perseverance as cheerful, to bypass getting caught in a grim sense of duty or of specialness.

Perseverance is no small thing, because at times our resistance can be very strong. Isn't it a fact that we often don't want to stay with our experience of what's going on in the present moment for more than a few seconds? So cultivating perseverance over the years is almost like building a muscle: we develop the strength and capacity without which meditation practice could never really develop. Basically, we learn that practice—or life—doesn't have to please us in the ordinary sense. Nor do we have to achieve a particular result in order to be able to continue.

In the phrase "cheerful perseverance is the key to success," what does *key* mean? This is particularly subtle, because perseverance is not the end in itself, in the sense of trying to fulfill an ideal of being dutiful in persevering. Rather, perseverance is the *catalyst*, the key that opens the door—the doorway to living genuinely. It is also "key" in the sense of crucial, in that perseverance is without doubt one of the most important qualities in a meditation practice. Without perseverance, meditation won't take root or blossom.

And *success*—what does that point to? This is the tricky part. It's not the same as in achieving a goal or the conventional cookie. Success is in the actual living of a more awake, freer life—no longer demanding that life be different. It ultimately means living more from the kindness, the gratitude, and the love

that are manifestations of our true nature. Cheerful perseverance is actually the means through which our aspiration can be
channeled—toward the possibility of living an authentic life.

During sitting in meditation, the quality of perseverance
is particularly key, because there are times when we just want
to get up and run out of there. And within sittings, perseverance means to try to stay present through the ups and downs
in moods. When we're bored, cheerful perseverance tells us to
just stay. It doesn't matter how we feel. All that matters is that
we can honestly acknowledge what is going on, and then stay
present as best we can.

The same is true with sleepiness: we don't have to fight it
or judge it. It's the small mind, the judgmental mind, that tells
us we're weak or wasting time or flunking at meditation. So we
simply feel what it feels like to be sleepy, and persevere, even if
the awareness is very low-key. And with physical or emotional
pain, cheerful perseverance means a willingness to just let it
in, to feel it, to reside in it, without trying to push it away or
make it better. No matter what we feel, no matter what comes
up for us, the practice is to clearly see the believed thoughts
and to truly feel and reside in the visceral experience of what
is—and then, with the breath and the environmental input as
our bigger context, to let our experience just be. If you think
you can't do that, just ask yourself if you can do it for at least
three full breaths. That's the start of perseverance.

Cheerful perseverance is the continuing effort to stay with
our meditation practice, even when we may question why we're
even doing it. In these times, perseverance particularly includes
not giving up on ourselves in our often messy efforts to work
with the muddiness and confusion of daily life. Perseverance
also builds the indispensable understanding that practice is

possible in just one place: in residing in exactly what we are experiencing *right now*. Learning to stay, to persevere, and to surrender to what is—these are the keys to the gateway to a lifelong meditation practice.

As we get older, meditation offers us one of the keys to experiencing a life of genuine equanimity. As we learn to reside in the stillness, the silence, of *just Being*, we taste the sweetness of *doing nothing*. This is not the same as laziness, or just trying to feel pleasure, or just lying around. Hedonism doesn't stay sweet for long, since it is rooted in trying to satisfy cravings that can never be completely satisfied. The deeper sweetness of doing nothing comes with being present with ourselves and with what life presents, rather than trying to stay busy or seek pleasure to fill up an inner absence or dissatisfaction. In fact, sitting in meditation is one of the few things that allow us to *just be*, even in the midst of discomfort.

When we can refrain from falling into the story line of our thoughts, whether they're based in the past or in the future—and instead attend to the immediacy of the physical experience of our life—we can connect with a sense of presence and openness. Regardless of our age or difficulties, we can experience a lightness of Being that makes living feel worthwhile.

Basic Meditation Instructions

If possible, it is best to meditate in the same place every day. Ideally, the space should be uncluttered and as quiet as possible.

It is also beneficial to meditate at the same time every day, to help foster the discipline necessary to overcome occasional laziness or loss of motivation. This helps to develop the necessary quality of perseverance.

Many people find it helpful to have a small altar. Lighting a candle or a stick of incense can help kindle our aspiration, as can having an inspirational picture or quotation on the altar.

Ideally, we sit in meditation every day. At the very least, sit three or four times a week. When you first begin your meditation practice, you may want to sit for just fifteen minutes, but in order to experience the full value of meditation, I suggest gradually increasing the time up to around thirty minutes (and more can be valuable too).

Whether you sit on a cushion or in a chair, it is helpful to sit in an erect but relaxed posture. Staying erect helps keep the mind alert, while staying relaxed helps prevent unnecessary strain. However, if conditions require that you lie down to meditate, the practice is to remain as still as possible, to allow a gradual settling down.

The eyes can be open or closed. The main time to keep the eyes open is when you're sleepy, since it's quite easy to enter into a dreamy state with the eyes closed. This may feel pleasant, but it is not conducive to being awake and aware, which is one of the main points of meditating.

Start by taking several deep, slow breaths to bring awareness into the body.

Then, to help settle the body and mind, bring a focused attention to the breath. Feel the specific physical sensations of the breath entering and leaving the body, focusing on the area in the center of the chest as the breath goes in and out. Stay present with the physical experience of breathing for as long as you can, being aware of the tendency to have the attention pulled away into thinking, daydreaming, or planning.

During a single sitting period, you may get pulled away into thinking hundreds of times. This is very human, and there is no need to judge yourself as a bad meditator. Instead, each and every time you catch yourself lost in the mind, simply return to the physical sensations of the breath.

Intermediate Instructions

In the early stages of a meditation practice, it is fine to follow the breath for the entire sitting period; but as the mind and body begin to feel settled, it is good to let awareness expand to include other sensations in the body, as well as input from the environment, such as sounds and the texture of the air. This allows us to move from a very concentrated awareness on just the breath to a more open state of awareness. This helps meditative attention move increasingly into daily life.

Since thoughts will no doubt continue to arise, the instruction is to notice them and then refrain from letting them play out by putting them on "call waiting." Then, return to awareness of the breath and the input from the environment.

When you find yourself caught in thoughts, it is helpful to renew the intention to come back to being present for at least the duration of three breaths. The first breath reestablishes awareness of the breath itself; the second reestablishes awareness of the environment; and the third reintroduces an overall awareness of the breath *and* the environment together. Even if you have to come back to these three breaths dozens of times during a sitting period, eventually the dual awareness of breath and environment will become the foundation of your meditation practice.

When strong emotions arise that demand your attention, instead of trying to ignore them or bypass them, bring awareness to the physical texture of the emotions, and then let them be included within the larger container of awareness of breath and environment. This will be discussed in more detail in the following chapters on working with the specific difficulties we encounter as we age, including anxiety, loss, helplessness, and physical pain.

Students often judge meditation periods as bad if they can't focus or if they don't feel good. Don't fall into this trap of judgment! In fact, one of the great benefits of meditation comes from persevering regardless of how we feel or what judgments arise. Eventually, a learning and a settling will begin to take place. And gradually, the sense of presence and equanimity that is cultivated through a daily meditation practice begins to stay with us throughout the day.

As we begin to experience the benefits of meditation—learning to relax deeply, as well as to feel more present—we will most likely want to prioritize meditation as a part of living in the natural monastery. Some days we may feel lazy and not want to do it; other days we may just want diversions. Still, as we increasingly understand that we don't have endless time, we start to pay more attention to our aspiration to spend our days doing what we realize is most important to us.

The more we practice meditation, the more we can experience an inner equanimity regardless of our outer circumstances. In this way, meditation becomes self-justifying, and as we get older, we can increasingly enjoy the fruit of feeling truly at home with ourselves and our circumstances, come what may.

PART II

Working with Difficulties

5

Anxiety and Depression

TO SOME DEGREE OR OTHER, anxiety, fear, and depression are with us intermittently through most of our lifetime—but they can be particularly difficult to deal with as we get older. While it's common at any age to experience anxiety when something goes wrong with our bodies, as we get older, each decline in our bodies can trigger an even stronger emotional response—including a sense of panic. Most often, however, it is the fear itself rather than the actual physical decline that will give us the most difficulty. Fear is always challenging, but when it leads us to imaginings of "the writing on the wall," it can easily turn into a sense of doom. Left unchecked, catastrophizing thoughts can lead to a chronic sense of despair and depression.

We're so used to judging states like fear and depression as "bad" that we often jump to the conclusion that something needs to be fixed. Our first thought may be to take medications to relieve the anxiety or depression. Resorting to medications may be okay as a temporary measure, especially during difficult periods—but relying on drugs for the long term may be problematic.

The good news is there are effective ways to work with fear and depression beyond the use of medications. First it's helpful to know the nature of what we're dealing with. The voice of fear tells us to turn away from whatever we perceive as dangerous,

73

but when we believe in and indulge this voice, we remain stuck in the narrow, protected cocoon world that fear creates. This is why fear is so difficult for us—not just because it feels bad in the moment, but because, under the guise of protecting us and keeping us safe, it prevents us from opening into life. Ironically, we cling to the belief that avoiding our fears can bring us happiness, yet exactly the opposite is true. The fearful thoughts are still running subliminally, so even as we try to avoid them, we stay quietly miserable.

It is also helpful to understand the nature and dynamics of depression. In a certain sense, depression can be viewed as a distorted way of trying to feel better, since depression dulls the emotions that we believe will make us unhappy—like hurt, sadness, and fear. Even if we believe that we don't want to be depressed, another part of us fears the discomfort of our buried feelings even more. Furthermore, depression is problematic because, as with fear, we erect walls to protect ourselves—walls that sap our aliveness, as we accept emotional numbness as a substitute for living. In order to learn to relate to our depression in a new way, we have to be willing to directly encounter our emotions—including the very ones that we don't want to feel.

For many of us, there are no doubt times that fear and depression will arise as we get older; and learning to relate to them in a new way is a necessity, especially because these painful states are often reinforced by the culturally accepted bias that the process of aging inevitably involves deterioration and dread. Holding these negative attitudes toward aging—seeing aging as a process of inevitable decline—can become a self-fulfilling prophecy, where we come to expect fear and depression as inevitable. The alternative is to see our difficult emotions from the view of the natural monastery, which includes learning to deal with states like fear and depression as part of our spiritual practice. This starts with the intention to refrain from accepting the view that aging equals failure.

The first step in working with our fears is to become clear about what we're actually afraid of, since we often don't know what we're really feeling or why exactly we are afraid.

Some time ago, I had four very short nightmares back to back in the same evening. They didn't require any analysis—their meaning was painfully obvious to me. They are the four classic faces of fear. In the first I was in the ocean, about waist-deep, and saw a ten-foot wave coming at me. I turned back toward the shore to get away, and saw a thirty-foot wave coming at me from the other direction. The fear here was obvious: fear of physical danger, pain, and loss of safety.

In the next dream I was waiting on a corner to be picked up. I didn't know who was picking me up, but the person was important to me. The person didn't show up, and as I waited, I noticed that there wasn't a single person anywhere in sight. The fear here was, as you might imagine, of abandonment, isolation, and loss of connection.

In the next one I was using a small massage tool for a painful headache and it stopped working—and when I tried to fix it, it shattered into thousands of pieces. The fear, of course, was of powerlessness and loss of control.

And in the last one, I was teaching a meditation class and most of the students were soundly sleeping. I yelled at the top of my lungs, "*Wake up!*" but everybody ignored me. The fear was of being unworthy and inadequate—and of no longer being relevant to the lives of others.

These four fears happen to be the four most universal fears: loss of safety, including fear of pain and physical danger;

abandonment and loss of connection, including fear of death; powerlessness and loss of control; and unworthiness. Most of the time what we're specifically afraid of isn't as obvious as it was with my nightmares. Anxiety or depression can creep in like fog, surrounding us and leaving us somewhat paralyzed, yet without even knowing what hit us. The first step in working with these difficult states is to recognize what's really going on.

When we have a vague idea that we're afraid, part of the power of fear is that it's still hiding in the shadows. To bring it out of the shadows, one simple, straightforward question can help, asking: *"What exactly am I afraid of?"* If the answer isn't clear, we can ask it again later. We just raise the question, and then go about our business, and at some point the answer is likely to reveal itself. Just naming a fear can sometimes weaken the dread of what the future will bring, and is the first step in working with our fears.

To be able to recognize our fears, it is helpful to look more closely at some of the most common ones. An almost universal fear as we age is the loss of safety and security. This can revolve around fear of pain and disease, or losing material security. Because safety is fundamental to our survival, this fear will often be triggered at the first sign of danger or insecurity, or when we experience new physical symptoms. In most cases, even when this fear is triggered, there may be no real danger to us; our fears are often imaginary, like believing that a dip in the stock market means that a loss of our life savings is imminent, or fearing that a feeling in our arm means we're having a heart attack, or that the discomfort in our stomach is proof we have cancer. Of course if a symptom persists, we get it checked out medically. Yet, until we see this dimension of fear with clarity, we will continue to live with a sense of constriction that can seem daunting.

Whatever fears we have from childhood, particularly the ones that stay with us through adulthood, will certainly continue as we get older. For example, when we start with a basic fear, like believing that we're not good enough, we're likely to develop a strategy of behavior to counter it, like the strategy of trying harder. We may have the basic belief: "If I try hard enough to prove myself, I won't have to feel the fear of worthlessness." Accordingly, we work very hard to be productive, to demonstrate our value, to excel in whatever we do. We may not even be aware how driven we are by the core fear of being unworthy. In fact, the need to bolster and maintain the self-image of success can be so strong that we may fool ourselves for a lifetime.

As we get older, we may not need or be able to be so productive or to prove ourselves in the ways we've been used to. Yet even having fewer responsibilities can leave us vulnerable to our fears in a new way. Since we no longer have access to some of the ways we've used to prove ourselves (i.e., being productive), we can no longer divert ourselves from feeling the fear driving our activities. Until the fear of not being good enough is addressed, it will continue to haunt us as we face new situations where we feel the need to demonstrate our worth. The same is true of the strategy of seeking approval. Seeking approval is natural—it's part of the survival mode of wanting to be liked in order to fit into the herd—but using approval seeking as a control strategy to mask our insecurities is not something we want to take with us to our grave, since it will only perpetuate our unhappiness.

Another significant fear that we need to recognize within ourselves is the fear of powerlessness and loss of control. This will often come into play when we get a severe diagnosis or when some major change in our bodies or health status occurs. When I was told I had a tumor on my kidney, after the initial shock and numbness, I experienced the inner sense of chaos that accompanies the feeling of powerlessness. At first I was vaguely aware of the anxiety, but I didn't know what I was really feeling on a deeper level. My immediate impulse was to go into action: getting another opinion, doing research on the internet—anything to avoid feeling the deeper sense of panic and dread. But again, until we can clearly see where we're caught in fear, we can't begin to free ourselves from its grip.

Just as with the fear of loss of safety, or unworthiness, or powerlessness and loss of control, our aging will no doubt bring us in increasing contact with the fear of the loss of loved ones, including the fear of abandonment and a loss of connection. This fear can be particularly powerful, and disguise itself in many forms, such as denial, anger, and especially depression. Sorting through what we're actually feeling may be difficult, but again, the first step is simply asking, "What exactly am I really afraid of?"

There are other fears that seem to be an integral part of the process of aging. For some there is the fear of death, and especially the fear of the pain and suffering that may be involved in dying. The fear of the loss of our mental faculties often becomes stronger as we age, and simply being unable to remember someone's name can trigger this fear. For many, the fear of having to deal with fear itself is perhaps the strongest fear—the aversion to feeling the intense, unpleasant sensations of anxiety and fear. Again, to free ourselves from these fears, we must first see them clearly within ourselves—bringing them out of the shadows.

Once we recognize clearly what we are specifically afraid of, the next step is something that may at first seem almost counterintuitive: seeing fear itself as our path to inner growth and freedom. Instead of viewing fear as our enemy, we can begin to see fear as a wake-up call, a signal. From the viewpoint of the natural monastery, fear presents us with an opportunity to see where we're stuck, where we're holding ourselves back, and where we can open more to life. We have to understand that fear is the protective cocoon of ego telling us to stop, to withdraw. Fear tells us not to go beyond the outer edge of our cocoon.

But the direction of the path toward inner freedom is to move directly toward our fears, since this is the only way to go beyond fear's cocoon. While we may not like it, fear can be our best indicator that we're going in the right direction. So instead of greeting fear with "Oh no!"—which is our reflexive response—we can say "Hello" to it, just like we would say hello to a friend. We can say, "Here you are again—what will you feel like this time?" The spiritual teacher Ram Dass often speaks of inviting fear in for a cup of tea, saying: "Fear of pain? Oh yeah— haven't seen you for a while. Tell me what's been happening." By relating *to* the fear rather than *from* it, being caught in it is substantially diminished.

Often when fear arises, we may think that dealing with it will automatically be a grim task—and believing this can engender a sense of resistance that leaves us with little motivation to move forward. But there's another way of looking at it. Fellow teacher Gregg Krech suggests that the antidote to saying "I *have* to work with fear" is to say "I *get* to work with fear." We see it as something that is actually helpful. We understand that we get to work with exactly what is holding us back from experiencing equanimity and freedom. So for me, when physical pain arises, I tell myself I *get to* work with it again—meaning I have an opportunity to work with my attachment to comfort, my attachment to my body, my attachment to my grim thoughts and to my fears—all of which prevent me from being free.

After all, if I didn't have the fear of pain to push me, I would never work with it in this crucial way. This is another way of seeing our fear as our path, but in a little lighter way. Maybe we can't quite muster, "Oh boy, I get to work with my fears," but we can nonetheless be willing to invite ourselves to be curious and to explore them. This can sometimes enable us to see fear more as an adventure than as a nightmare.

The actual practice is to *pause*, and allow ourselves to observe the thoughts racing through our mind. It's tempting, when fear arises, to start to think and analyze; in fact, thinking is likely inevitable. But indulging in it, by letting the repetitive thoughts continue to run, is optional. We can always take a step back and just watch what the mind is doing, and how it tries to solidify the thoughts into suffering—by exacerbating the fear and/or aversion to it. It is also helpful to ask ourselves, *"What is actually going on right now?"* Often there is nothing going on in the present moment that is frightening, yet our thoughts tell us to be afraid. So it's good to be clear on the difference between what is really happening and what we're thinking could happen. Then we can examine our thoughts, by seeing them objectively, and recognize that they are only thoughts—not reality.

One way to become aware of the specific beliefs that are part of our fears is to ask ourselves the following question: *"What is my most believed thought?"* This question can point us to something important that may be just below the level of awareness—quite often a deeply held, unexamined core story we're taking as truth. But just because we believe it doesn't make it true.

One of my students mentioned how she wakes up every morning with the feeling of a heavy weight on her chest. After asking the question, "What is my most believed thought?" she realized her first thought was always, "It's not supposed to be this way!" Similarly, I remember a long period through my forties waking up every day with an anxious quiver in my stomach.

No thought was apparent, but after asking, "What is my most believed thought?" I saw that the anxious feelings were always accompanied by the thought, "This is just too hard. I can't do it!" Both of these examples point to the power of our conditioned thinking, of which we're often unaware. And as we get older, that conditioning will not simply go away on its own; it must be addressed directly.

When it's especially difficult to see where we're caught in our conditioned thinking, there's a very effective technique called *mind mapping*. Here's how it works.

If you are stuck in an emotional issue and unclear about what you're actually thinking or feeling, first think of a short phrase which best describes the issue; then write that phrase down in the middle of a piece of paper and circle it. For example, it could say, "Relationship Difficulty," "Depression," or "Anxiety over Health." Next write down the first few thoughts that come to mind. Then, over the next few hours or days, whenever a thought, emotion, or strong bodily sensation arises around the issue, write it down on the paper. The entries don't have to be in any order—you can scatter them all over the page. Basically, you're creating a map of the mind, letting all of the debris that keeps floating through the mind be objectified on paper: emotions and sensations, as well as thoughts, are included.

It's important in this exercise to refrain from *analyzing* the issue or trying to somehow fix it. Instead of trying to figure out what's going on, the practice is to objectively observe the thoughts and feelings—and write them down. Don't think too hard about what to write—just let whatever is there pour onto the page unhindered. The point of simply writing the items down is to be able to eventually *see* with real clarity what you are believing and feeling on both conscious and subconscious levels.

Once you have written down most of the thoughts and feelings (this may take place over the course of a few hours or even days), look at the whole page as if you were looking at a map of your mind. Notice any repeating patterns of thoughts, and also notice the relationship between the thoughts and the emotional and physical feelings. At this point, ask yourself the pivotal practice question, "What is the most believed thought?"

There's a good chance the answer will not be apparent immediately, since often the thoughts we write down are superficial or surface thoughts. Repeat this question again, either right away or sometime later; if you are intent on knowing what you're believing, the chances are strong that sooner or later the answer will present itself with clarity.

Once the most believed thought becomes apparent, add it to the map of the mind. At this point, when you look at the overall map, it almost always becomes clear how the surface thoughts and also the emotional feelings rose directly from that initial belief. Deeply held beliefs like "Life is too hard," "I'll always be alone," or "Nothing will ever work out" may sound trite, but their devastating power becomes apparent the more we get to know ourselves—as we observe how these thoughts dictate how we feel and act.

The point of practicing mind mapping is to be able to *see* our anxiety and depression within a wider container of awareness. When we can see ourselves and our difficult situation more clearly, we are no longer likely to believe the small mind's thoughts and judgments. Being able to see that these thoughts and emotions are not "me" is pivotal in being able to become free of them.

We may find that many of the fearful thoughts focus on worrying about the future. They can even act like radar, where what we perceive is determined by what we're looking for. If we're irrationally worried about getting cancer, for instance, our radar will focus on even benign physical symptoms as proof that we probably have cancer. There was a Woody Allen character who thought he had cancer on his back until it was pointed out to him that it was just a spot on his shirt. Absurd, yes, but if we let our worrying about the future run unchecked, it can turn into full-blown catastrophizing, where everything seems dark and unworkable.

The stories fears tell us can seem *real*, and cause us unnecessary distress over a situation that isn't even happening and may, in fact, never happen. If it's clear that there is no real danger on board at the moment, a good way to break the cycle of fear is to say, "*Not happening now!*" We may have to repeat this phrase a few times when unrealistic mental scenarios take hold, and although it is only a temporary solution, this practice will usually clear the mind of fear-based catastrophic thinking for long enough that life may no longer seem so dark and unworkable.

At other times our fear-based thoughts can become obsessive—so strong that they take on a life of their own. Each time we indulge the obsessive thoughts, it's like throwing a log on a fire. So to let the fire die out, each and every time apocalyptic thoughts arise we can cut them off by saying, "*Don't go there!*" We may have to say this several times, but it will generally cut the obsessive loop and bring us back to a degree of clarity.

Then there are times that our obsessive fear-based thoughts become so strong that even saying "Don't go there!" may not help. In these instances you can try a particular breathing technique, which works on an energetic level. Breathe in for four seconds, hold the breath for four seconds, and then forcefully expel the breath. Do this three times, and the energetic-based thought pattern will most likely be broken. If not, repeat the process a few times as necessary.

The point of working with the thoughts that the spinning mind keeps churning out is to enable us to drop whatever story line we're caught in. Once we can refrain from indulging in thoughts such as "This is awful," "I can't handle this," or "Poor me," the melodrama begins to lose its steam. After we can dis-identify with the surface thoughts, the next and crucial step is to feel the physical sensations and energy of fear throughout our body. We do this by breathing right into them—which gives them a little ventilation or breathing room.

Basically we're asking the pivotal question *"What is this?"*— which means "What does this moment actually feel like, in the body?" We're not asking why we have fear or analyzing it; it isn't an intellectual question. Instead, it's a way to enter meticulously into the body sensations on a felt level. You notice where, specifically, the sensations are strongest, and then feel their texture.

For me, with anxiety, I feel it mostly in the chest and stomach. It usually feels queasy and quivery. So the question "What is this?" is an experiential way of dealing with anxiety and fear. And again, we follow this by breathing into the bodily sensations.

It may also be helpful to breathe the physical feelings and energy of fear into the center of the chest for a few breaths. There is definitely something soothing and healing about bringing the fear to the area of the heart and simply feeling that area. We may find that our usual dread is replaced with a genuine curiosity. As our fears begin to dissolve, we may begin to naturally tap into the connectedness and love that are always available to us. These are the real fruit of willingly engaging our fears. You need to try this for a while to actually experience the benefit.

We can work with depression using the same step-by-step

process that we did with fear. We start by becoming clearly aware that we are, in fact, depressed. Often, we don't even know it. Paraphrasing Kierkegaard, the precise character of depression is that it does not realize it is depression. Also, with depression, we may not be motivated to work with it, because one of the attributes of depression is that motivation is often very low. The trick is to try to view the depression with the curiosity of a scientist—as something to study objectively. In a way, this is a subtle version of seeing the depression as your path. The idea is that, by studying the thoughts and feelings that constitute the depression, it will become increasingly less solid, thereby freeing us from its somber grip.

To study the depression with curiosity, we start by objectively looking at what the mind is believing. Asking, *"What is my most believed thought?"* will no doubt turn up some versions of: *"I'm no good"* or *"What's the point?"* or *"Everything's hopeless."* Just naming these thoughts takes away at least some of their power.

Then we ask the question *"What is this?"*—bringing curiosity to what we're feeling in the body. Is it heaviness? Where do we feel it? What does the heaviness actually feel like? By entering into the body in this way, we are breaking our identification with the depression as being who we are. I don't mean to make this sound easy—it's likely to take repeated efforts. It may also require using the phrases *"Not happening now!"* and *"Don't go there!"* But the dual process of clearing the mind and settling into the body will eventually begin to lift the heaviness of the depression.

Both of these approaches—of seeing our thoughts clearly and physically feeling what is going on in the body—are enhanced as we cultivate the mindset of greeting challenges like fear and depression by literally saying Yes to them. Saying Yes is not merely a can-do attitude or an affirmation—which will inevitably fall short in the face of some of the harsh realities of aging. Saying Yes is about a willingness to truly feel our present moment experience. This mindset grows as we're increasingly unwilling to stay complacent. Saying Yes allows us to move toward unknown territory, even when the voices of fear and depression tell us to not go there. As we come to understand that without this step we will forever remain stuck, there's a willingness to enter into life in a new way.

Sometimes we may think we can't say Yes. When we find ourselves in the midst of such a painful or distressing experience, usually it is very difficult to stay present with it. This is normal, because as humans, we have a natural aversion to discomfort, and as a consequence our resistance can be very strong. The voice of fear tells us we have reached an edge beyond which we're unable to go. The voice of depression simply says no.

And yet our aspiration tells us to take one more step forward. While our unhealed emotions may warn us to close down and defend, the heart that wants to awaken says yes—it calls us to open up and connect with what life is actually presenting. Until we become intimate with our fears and depression, until we can welcome them, they will always limit our ability to live authentically. Saying Yes to life means saying Yes to everything, even fear and depression. In other words, the path to the truly genuine life requires our openhearted attention to the very things that seem to block our way to it.

Regardless of what we do, there may be times when the experience of fear and depression feels too strong to stay with. When this occurs, we can take deep relaxing breaths, as in the deep breathing meditation—where we breathe in slowly through the nose and breathe out slowly through the slightly open mouth. When the fear or depression is really too strong to stay with in any way, we can also temporarily find distractions. With depression, for example, just taking a walk outside—which we may initially resist doing—may help the depression lift. This too is part of the bigger tent of the natural monastery, as long as we don't abuse it. Sometimes it's difficult to know when we should take it easy and when we should try a little harder—this may be different for each one of us. But learning this is part of the art of growing older with wisdom.

Ultimately, we can see that our fear and depression are actually just a collection of conditioned beliefs and intense body sensations. This is how we come to the critical understanding that even while these emotions might remain, we do not have to identify with them as being the truth, or who we are. This is what it means to be free from them: it's not that they're no longer present (which may be impossible), but they decreasingly dictate who we are or how we live.

The real question is this: Can our aspiration to live authentically become more important than indulging the stories of fear and depression?

Eventually, we all need to be willing to face the deepest, darkest beliefs we have about ourselves. Only in this way can we come to *know* that they are only *beliefs*—and not reality. By willingly entering into this process, we can see through the fiction of who we believe ourselves to be.

Love is the fruit of saying Yes, of consciously and willingly facing both our fears and our depression. Once consciously faced, they no longer block the love that is our true nature from coming forth freely on its own.

6

Grief and Loss

Grief

As we get older there is no way to avoid the experience of grief.

We will lose our friends, and often, our life partner. So much has been written about the five stages of grief, or some version of them, that many now speak about grief with an ease or a certainty that leaves me perplexed. My own experience of grief doesn't fit neatly into any formula. In fact, grief can manifest in so many different ways that it almost defies a clear description. At the same time it is one of the most intense and real emotions that we will ever experience. Grief, along with loss in general, is one of the most difficult experiences that we will ever have to go through.

I'm in my early seventies, so it's natural that many people in my life have already died. The deaths that affected me the most were five of my closest friends, including my former wife—all of whom died relatively young. Two of them died in their forties, suddenly and with no warning. I had known one of them since kindergarten; we went through school together, were college roommates for four years, and later I built a home for him and his family. Then shortly after he turned forty he took his own life, and when I heard the news, I was so shaken that I broke down every day, sometimes uncontrollably, for several weeks.

In part, my grieving was the realization of how much pain he had to be in to do what he did. But a large part of it, I realized later, was not just for the loss of someone I cared deeply about—but for something inside of me that seemed to have gotten lost as well. My (not necessarily conscious) view of the world was that there was a stability and certainty that I could count on. There was also the belief (again not conscious) that I myself had endless time. My friend's death shattered these illusions, and the sense of groundlessness shook my feelings of complacency. But as intense as my feelings were, after a time my former sense of control returned, although now with a little less certainty.

My other friend who died young had been my closest friend for twenty-five years; he was the one person I could talk to about anything and feel understood. In his late forties, he had a sudden and massive heart attack while playing basketball. He died instantly, and when I was given the news, I was unable to even take it in. At the time I was in the middle of a several months' long acute flare-up of an autoimmune disorder. I didn't have the energy or strength to process the feelings, so for two months, until I started to get better, I buried them. Then, as my strength returned, the deep waves of sadness and loss rose to the surface. Fortunately, by then I was able to process the grief in a way that deepened my heart, and also connected me more deeply with the grief that we all share. I will speak about this process a little later in the chapter.

I learned that even though someone dies, they still can have a very profound place in the heart. For many years after his death I silently talked to him every day—sharing my life with him as if he were still there. It's not that I believed he could literally hear me, it was more the sense of connectedness that survives the loss of the body.

Each experience of grief has hit me differently.

I was with my mother in the hospital when she was diagnosed with lymphoma, with a poor prognosis. While I was with her, I was able to maintain a calm presence for her, but as soon as I left the hospital it felt like I had been punched in the stomach. I remember having to lean against the brick wall of the hospital—the same building where I had been born fifty-three years earlier—and feeling like my tether to the earth was being disconnected. There's no way to prepare for an experience like that; as with aging, we're all beginners when it comes to dealing with grief. We may not even know what we're feeling or what to do with it.

Grief is difficult to feel because it's often both intense and constantly changing. Sometimes it manifests as anger, sometimes as fear, often as sadness and dread. Sometimes grief arises at the most seemingly unlikely times—when we hear a bird singing or see a flower in bloom. Often one small moment of grief taps into other griefs—the layers of unresolved pain that we've been avoiding—such as fears of separation, abandonment, and insecurity. Grief can make us feel heavy or weary, empty or incomplete, terrified or despairing. No wonder it often manifests as numbness that freezes out the feelings of separation and isolation that we don't want to feel. Within grief there is almost always the insecurity of losing an anchor, as I felt when my mother was diagnosed with cancer—the feeling of groundlessness that comes when it seems there is nothing to hold on to. And always within grief there is longing—for wholeness, for completion, for harmony, for connection.

From my own experiences and also from working with others, I've learned that there's no way to truly anticipate the intensity of the feelings of grief. When someone we love dies, the loss can sometimes seem unbearable. The closer we are, especially when we have become "glued at the hip" to one another, the more painful the loss. Often the mind cannot accept it—the belief, "This was not supposed to happen!" can stay with us for weeks and even months or years. The days can seem empty; the thought of tomorrow or next week can leave us feeling numb or disheartened; birthdays, holidays, and particularly anniversaries can make us feel raw all over again.

For a time grief can become our whole existence—the feelings of pain and emptiness may be all that we know. But over time, we usually gain some distance from our feelings, particularly as we allow the feeling to pass through the heart. The intensity begins to lessen, and sometimes we even forget we're grieving. Then at times it may come back full bore. Someone described this experience like the ocean, with the waves of grief at first being large and frequent, pushing us down to the ocean floor. Unable to hold our breath, it feels as if we will drown. Then the waves subside, and we can come up for air. As time passes so do the currents, and the waves become smaller and less frequent, although occasionally a large wave will come out of nowhere and knock us back down again. But by then we have learned that we will not drown.

One of the main pitfalls of grieving is that we can begin to wallow in it. In fact, the ego can usurp the genuine feelings, and grieving can become a whole new identity. We see ourselves primarily as "a grieving person"—and the feeling of being a victim or a martyr overshadows our genuine sadness. When this happens, instead of learning from our grief it can become a prison. On the opposite end, instead of wallowing in our grief we can suppress it, in the hope that we won't have to feel the pain. But as psychologist and author John Welwood insightfully observed, "What we fail to grieve turns into grievance." This is common, since anger is so much easier to access than the emotion of grief. Anger, after all, can give us a seductive feeling of power and of being in control, so it's easy to become lost in forms of anger like frustration, resentment, and bitterness.

The key to learning from our grief is realizing that we don't need to resist it. As painful as it may be, when we allow ourselves to truly feel it, it can open us in a way that few other things can. And there's a very specific practice that is particularly effective in helping us process our grief. The practice, which I adopted from one of Stephen Levine's meditations, is to "breathe into the heart." Of course we don't actually breathe into the heart, but on the in-breath, we breathe *as if* we're breathing directly into the center of the chest.

Here are the instructions.

Breathing into the Heart

Sitting or lying down, take a few deep breaths to bring awareness into the body.

Place three fingertips on the chest center, against the sternum; you may find a tender or sore spot on the sternum, but anywhere in this area in the middle of the chest is fine.

Press in slightly, feeling whatever sensitivity may be there. At the very least you will feel the sensations of the fingers against the sternum.

Become aware of the breath, and as you breathe in, feel whatever sensations arise where your fingers rest on the chest.

Imagine you are breathing *as if* the breath is entering the body through the heart center, almost as if there were a conduit right into the heart area.

Continue breathing in this way for just a minute or two, but come back to it periodically throughout the day, until it feels natural to breathe into the heart.

Eventually it may feel very refreshing and enlivening, as if the breeze were going right through you.

Once you learn this practice—and it takes a little while to get used to it—it can be helpful in processing the feelings of grief, as well as sadness and loneliness. When we're grieving, this area in the center of the chest is sometimes so sensitive that when we press it with our fingers, we can feel the tenderness or soreness.

The actual practice is to use the in-breath to breathe the physical sensations and energy of grief directly into this point in the center of the chest. We may feel it as heaviness, an ache, or tightness in the throat. Then, on the out-breath, we softly release the breath. We're not trying to do anything with our experience of grief other than let it in.

Perhaps the only word that can describe the process of opening into grief is *surrender.* We're not trying to transform it, and we're not trying to let it go. Rather, by breathing it into the center of the chest we're inviting ourselves to experience grief in a new way, within the context of the spaciousness of the heart. Although at times these sensations can feel like they may paralyze us, the truth is they can deepen our ability to meet our grief with compassion. When we do this, we're no longer caught in the thinking mind that tends to lament. Breathing grief into the chest center somehow, slowly, transforms the feelings; what may at first seem like unbearable pain gradually feels more like poignancy. And even when the pain remains, it can become more of an experience to be felt, rather than something that seems overwhelming.

When we allow ourselves to truly feel our grief, we will find that it can clear the mind like nothing else. It can show us what matters and what doesn't. It allows us to finally give up the illusion that we have all the time in the world, and we can begin to focus on living in a more genuine way—following our heart rather than living from *should* or old patterns that no longer serve us.

Grief has now become our teacher.

Loss

Aging and loss so often come together that they can seem almost synonymous. Loss arises through many situations, not just when someone we love dies. In fact, we all carry with us accumulated grief, which remains, sometimes unconsciously, from every situation that has ever invoked an intense emotional reaction to losing something. Each time we've felt loss—of a relationship, of a pet, of our ideals and dreams—it's common to bury the feelings and erect a layer of armor to protect us from feeling groundlessness, despair, and isolation.

But it gets more difficult to bury our feelings as we age, when it can seem as if life is one loss after another—and we can feel this acutely when we begin to lose our physical strength and stamina. We may feel loss even more intensely as our health begins to fail, or if we experience the beginnings of mental decline. Some may feel loss strongly when they lose their work, or a sense of place and importance. Those who experience divorce in their later years may feel loss, which sometimes appears as anger over the dissolution of ideals, or sadness at the loss of a sacred bond. Those who lose faith in their religion, especially after relying on it for support, can experience emptiness and uncertainty.

Anyone who has seen their heroes or idols falter or fall has experienced the feelings of sadness and incompleteness that are part of loss; when someone we admire dies, often our grief is magnified by the loss of our dreams that we may now fear will never be fulfilled.

When the pain of loss arises, we always have the choice to try to ward it off or bury it—or finally let it in. It's no wonder that we so often choose to push it away, since we have a natural aversion to feeling the strong and often unpleasant sensations that come with loss. We often turn to culturally acceptable ways to avoid feeling the pain. We might force ourselves to "be strong," or accept the notion that "God works in mysterious ways." But taking *any* position that prevents us from honestly facing what's really going on is just another way of burying our feelings. It's one more way of erecting the armor of a protective shield that we hope can keep us from feeling the pain of loss and grief. Back when we erected these barriers, we might have needed them, since at the time we might not have been able to open up to the intensity of our feelings. Protecting ourselves in this way was perhaps a good thing. But if we wish to live more genuinely, experiencing the spaciousness and equanimity of a more open heart, we need to be able to open fully into loss.

This will undoubtedly be difficult at times, but when we experience loss after loss, it has the power to awaken our aspiration to live wholeheartedly in a way that few other circumstances can. Loss can jolt us straight into realizing how much of our life has been wasted on trivialities. We begin to see the pettiness of our attitudes and opinions, and we understand the degree to which we've just been skating on thin ice. We appreciate that time is swiftly passing and, with it, our only chance of awakening to an authentic life. Rethinking our priorities, we're no longer so intent on clinging to our protections. We're no longer so interested in preserving comfort and safety as our gods—and we see that they haven't really been able to protect us. As we begin to feel the magnitude of how painful it is to hold back our hearts in fear, we become more willing to allow the intensity of loss into our experience.

As with experiencing grief, the most genuine way to process the experience of loss is through the practice of breathing the specific sensations and feelings of loss into the center of the chest. At first this may be difficult, and we may experience a lot of resistance, fearing that doing this will increase our pain. But with the clear understanding that we don't have endless time, coupled with the clear intention to live more honestly, the resistance will diminish.

And yet, even when the resistance is no longer such a barrier, there is still the greater barrier of our ceaselessly spinning minds, particularly the part of the mind that constantly judges our experience. In order to truly feel the experience of loss we first have to get out of the head, which tells us that what we're feeling is "terrible" or "too much" or "unfair." We can learn to observe these thoughts with precision, and as best we can, we put them aside. This is not the same as burying our feelings since it is our thoughts, not our feelings, that we are putting aside. This becomes easier as we begin to learn that *these thoughts are just thoughts*, and may have little to do with what is true. This is not to say that loss isn't painful, but there is a big difference between the thought, "This is *painful*" and "This is *terrible*." In fact, the latter places an additional layer of pain on top of what's already there. Identifying these disabling thoughts brings them out of the shadows, and they begin to lose their power; it's at this point that we can begin the practice of directly feeling the experience of loss.

Breathing as if we're breathing into the heart is described previously. If you haven't tried this, it's helpful to experiment with it for several sessions, simply as a breathing meditation, before trying to apply it to processing the feelings of loss. Once you feel comfortable with breathing into the heart, you can take the next step of using the in-breath to breathe the physical sensations and energy of loss directly into the center of the chest. We breathe the aching sensations of loss into the chest center and simply let them be there. Then, on the out-breath, we softly release the breath. With each in-breath we go a little bit deeper. All we're trying to do is feel the loss as fully as we can and rest in the experience. This is the process of surrender.

Sometimes we may be able to rest in our pain without struggle. Other times, all we may be able to do is feel it for a few breaths. In fact, there's a practice—called *The Three Breaths Practice*—which is especially useful when we're not able to go deeper.

The Three Breaths Practice

When we recognize that this is one of those times that it's too much to work with loss, we can intentionally decide to just feel the bodily sensations that come along with loss for the duration of three breaths.

The resistant ego is very likely to accept this, since it will not feel threatened, given it is for such a short time. And once we finish doing the three breaths, we honor our agreement and don't push any harder.

Then later we can come back again, and again, even if only three breaths at a time.

Many have found this practice is the perfect tool for those times when the experience of loss feels a little too overwhelming.

Breathing the sensations and feelings of loss into the center of the chest will gradually become more and more doable and comfortable. Even when it is still painful, there can be a kind of equanimity when we simply surrender to the feelings and let them in. How this all works is a mystery, but using the "heart's breath" to process the experience of loss allows what may have previously felt unbearable to actually be welcomed at times. Again, the pain may still remain, but now there's a sweetness or a poignancy that comes from the heart being more open to what the moment presents.

Sometimes, especially with the intense experience of grief, it is helpful to see our experience within a larger perspective.

When Elizabeth and I visited the remains of the concentration camp at Auschwitz, it was a very sobering experience. Before we left I picked up a handful of small stones from the mostly barren grounds and brought them home with me. I started the practice of carrying one of the stones in my pocket, and when I would find myself caught in emotional distress, I would put my hand in my pocket and feel the stone—reminding myself of the universality of human suffering. At one point I put one of the stones on the table right beside me where I have consultations with students, and sometimes when a student would describe their difficulties, after talking to them for a while, I would give them the stone—telling them how I use mine. My hope was that it would serve as a reminder of the suffering we all share, and perhaps somewhat ease the experience of distress they were feeling. We don't have to have a stone from a concentration camp as a reminder; we could use any stone or artifact that has some personal meaning for us. The point is to be able to bring a somewhat larger perspective to what we're feeling.

This is certainly not to say that experiencing loss will be easy or that all losses are equal. Some losses may feel as if they knock us to the ground. For example, it is natural as we get older for our sexual desires to gradually diminish. For many, especially men, this can feel as if our life is over, like our last vestige of youth is now gone. After I had surgery for kidney cancer, I had to be catheterized for several weeks, and for over two months having sex was out of the question. I had never even considered this before—I apparently had the unconscious belief that I would be able to continue having sex indefinitely.

At first the thought of not having sex again was a big blow—like something essential to my being was possibly gone forever. But as I breathed the acute feelings of loss into the chest center, something shifted in my understanding. I realized that far from my life now being a failure, I still had the possibility for genuine intimacy with Elizabeth, and perhaps on an even deeper level. By acknowledging the possibility that we could no longer have the same kind of sexual relationship, and surrendering to the feelings of loss, I actually accepted it, and, to my great surprise, was truly okay with it. I also felt a sincere and heartfelt willingness to move in a different direction—toward a new kind of intimacy. Happily for me my ability to have sex returned, but I learned something important, and gave up at least a little of my attachment to my body.

With each loss we are given the opportunity to become free of our attachments. If we lose our ability to have sex or lose our partner, we may gradually become more free of our attachment to our sexual desires, and instead channel our attention to creative activities that we might not have previously undertaken, like writing, art, gardening, or whatever we might feel we formerly missed out on doing. Or we could channel our attention into new friendships, finding a different kind of connection than physical intimacy. With the loss of our youthful appearance—

where we have to accept that we are getting grayer or more wrinkled—we have the opportunity to work on our attachment to the need to appear appealing. As we breathe this sense of loss into the heart center, we may come to the very freeing realization that the need to appear appealing simply doesn't matter. What a relief! The same may be true with our deep attachment to feeling youthful. Certainly having more energy and stamina feels better than being tired, but as we work with what we sometimes think of painfully as our "lost youth," we may begin to appreciate our newfound ability to slow down and simply be—something that is rarely possible when we have the energy to stay constantly on the go.

Even if each loss sometimes feels as if it takes the ground out from under us, and each successive loss can make us feel as if it's harder to get up, as we work with these things, by breathing them into the chest center and feeling them fully, something transforms in our Being.

With each attachment that loosens its grip, the heart becomes a little more open, and instead of living in lament and self-pity, we may find ourselves living with a new lightness and a renewed appreciation for life. Although aging and loss are without doubt difficult, it is also true that sometimes our most difficult experiences are the ones that enrich us the most. One key is perseverance—or simply not giving up.

One of my favorite aphorisms, even if it's perhaps been over-used, is still a great reminder: "Seven times down, eight times up."

7

Loneliness and Helplessness

Loneliness

IN THE LAST YEARS OF OUR LIFE we may come face-to-face for the first time with the fact that we are, in some fundamental sense, alone. We can feel alone even when others are present, and even though we may have spent most of our life in close relationships, in the end it may become frightening clear that we may have to endure our last years being primarily alone. And we may even die alone. Indeed, this aloneness, this loneliness, can certainly be one of the most difficult aspects of getting older.

It is said that we are all born alone and that we all die alone, and in between it is our connectedness with others that takes the edge off of our basic aloneness. Yet, even within an intimate and healthy long-lasting relationship there will still always be a gap between oneself and another. As author Scott Turow put it, "How do we ever know what's in another's heart or mind? If we are always a mystery to ourselves, then what is the chance of understanding anybody else?"

This gap, which accounts for the existential isolation we may sometimes feel, is, on one level, unbridgeable—and honesty in the face of our aging may require that we acknowledge our basic aloneness. At times, all of us may feel fundamentally alone, and until we face this loneliness directly, we will fear it. It's interesting that one of life's most vital lessons is something we are rarely taught: how to be at home with ourselves. The philosopher Pascal said that much of man's misery derives from not being able to sit in a quiet room alone.

Most people will do almost anything to avoid the fear of loneliness. We distract ourselves, get busy, or look for escapes. We can even use our relationships to run away from feeling this fear. Ultimately, however, the willingness to come to terms with one's loneliness is an essential aspect of aging with equanimity.

This doesn't mean we can't still rely on relating to others for comfort and enjoyment. After all, human beings have an innate need for social contact—and if we ignore this need we may suffer unnecessarily in isolation. For those who find themselves alone after a death or divorce, or those who might have a tendency to isolate, it's important to be wary of building walls to protect ourselves from possible pain. Unless we can drop the walls of protection we will continue to experience the unhappiness of feeling separate and lonely. Part of the wisdom of getting older is finding people and activities that fulfill our need for human contact, without resorting to superficial attempts to fill up time. Relationships and social activities have to feel genuine if they are to be truly satisfying.

I was a volunteer at hospice for a period of ten years. My job was to sit with patients, or sometimes their spouses, in the patients' last months of life. With some of my hospice patients, I witnessed how that basic aloneness was softened by the ability of another to be truly present with them as the end came closer. To experience the sense of connection that comes through the presence of another is part of the wisdom that may be revealed as we near our end; it is to understand the paradox that, although we are basically alone, we are at the same time truly connected.

Even though we may fear being lonely, it doesn't mean we can't still enjoy being by ourselves or being quiet. Enjoying solitude can be wonderful, although often it doesn't take long for the urge for activity or entertainment to arise. We can watch this urge when it arises and choose to follow it, or we can notice it and return to and remain in solitude. The capacity to be alone is essential in transforming the pain of loneliness into the settledness of solitude—that is, of being at home with oneself. And yet, when loneliness hits us, the ability to feel at home in our own skin will not come to us naturally.

When we experience loneliness, perhaps the main thing we feel is isolated and separate, and this can be painful. It can trigger our deepest fears of not being enough or not being connected. We may realize that our need for another person is in part to have someone to witness our life, someone we can tell our ongoing story to. Without their presence we may feel emptiness—the feeling that we don't really exist, don't really matter, or perhaps that we are not loved. If we don't have our story and someone to hear it, we may feel shaken and begin to question whether our life has meaning.

When we no longer cover our loneliness with busyness and with our roles, there may arise the deepest existential question—what *is* my life really about? After all, for many years our story has defined who we are and what our value is. Without our story we will no doubt feel anxiety; yet one of the great benefits of aging is that we can get more in touch with what's truly important, which transcends our story. When we begin to question our life direction, rather than choosing old patterns like idle social interactions, we may choose our social activities with more intention. This means we don't speak just to speak, but instead converse about things that we find more meaningful.

The ability to speak and live with conscious intention isn't something that is given to us as a gift simply because we are getting older. Without reflection and effort, aging will most likely guarantee a continuation of whatever habits and reactions we've been repeating up until now. And it's very unlikely that these will help alleviate the pain of loneliness.

There's a specific practice that many have found helpful when faced with difficult emotions like loneliness. Elizabeth named this practice RRR—an abbreviation for *recognize, refrain, and return*. Simply put, first we must *recognize* what, specifically, we are feeling, and the "story of me" that may be repeating. Sometimes it's not so clear—because loneliness can feel like antsiness or boredom, and then morph into depression. So the first step is to recognize with clarity that the underlying feeling is in fact loneliness.

The second step is to *refrain*. Refrain from what? Primarily we want to refrain from allowing our thoughts to run rampant—thoughts such as: "It wasn't supposed to be this way." "This is too much to bear." "Why go on?" When we find ourselves spinning with thoughts like these, we can use the phrase, *"Don't go there!"* as a way of cutting through the mental spin cycle. But it's important to understand that this is not the same as suppression, since we are not cutting off our feelings; we're only setting aside the thoughts that tend to immerse us in wallowing. Once we can put space between ourselves and our thoughts we can go to the third *R*, which is to *return*.

What do we return to? We return to the present moment of loneliness, starting with feeling exactly what bodily sensations are present. Remember, in *refraining* we only turned away from the *thoughts* that exacerbate our loneliness, yet we didn't suppress our physical feelings. This makes it possible to truly feel what we're feeling, even if it's intense or painful. And the way we do this is with the "heart's breath."

Just as we did in working with grief and loss, we follow the in-breath into the center of the chest, and with each successive in-breath we breathe the sensations of loneliness into the chest center. Then, on the out-breath, we softly release. By breathing the sensations of loneliness into the heart, and by allowing ourselves to feel them fully, the experience of loneliness can gradually transform into something very different. Over time, although we may still be alone, we are no longer lonely. In this solitude there is an equanimity, and a clearer sense of our place in the world. A quote from Pema Chödrön, the well-known Tibetan Buddhist meditation teacher, is right on point: "Only to the extent that we expose ourselves over and over to annihilation can that which is indestructible in us be found."

The practice of *recognize, refrain, and return*, combined with breathing our emotions into the chest center, takes perseverance—and rarely will we feel any significant change with just a few attempts. But it can be difficult to stay with RRR for extended periods, so it can be helpful to combine it with a very different but complementary practice, called *reflective walking*. Reflective walking is an offshoot of a walking meditation taught by Vietnamese Zen teacher Thich Nhat Hanh. This practice is ideally done outside if possible, where we can relate to the air and plants and outdoor sounds. It's also best done fairly slowly, as if walking casually through a park. The actual practice involves reflecting on four short lines as we walk, bringing attention not only to the lines, but also staying aware of our inner and outer environment.

The lines I've been using for many years are:

> As I walk the mind will wander.
> With each sound the mind returns.
> With each breath the heart is open.
> With each step I touch the earth.

Each line is a reflection, and each line also directs our attention. The first line, "As I walk the mind will wander," is a description of what the mind actually does. If we're lonely, the mind will most likely wander into thoughts of loneliness and self-pity. The second line, "With each sound the mind returns," reminds us to let awareness return to what we're actually feeling, while also sensing our surroundings, particularly the sounds. The third line, "With each breath the heart is open," directs our attention to the breath into the center of the chest, and if we feel able, we gently breathe the sensations of loneliness (not the thoughts and stories about it!) into the chest center. The last line, "With each step I touch the earth," directs our attention to the fact that we don't have endless time, and is a reminder to appreciate that we can still walk on the earth and hear and breathe.

If we are unable to walk, this meditation can be adapted to sitting or lying down by simply changing the lines.

> As I sit the mind will wander.
> With each sound the mind returns.
> With each breath the heart is open.
> With each breath I feel alive.

Reflective walking can be done anytime, but it's a good complement to the more intense and difficult practice of RRR. Alternating these two keeps the practice of working with loneliness from becoming too heavy or grim. Just being outside, or wherever walking is possible, can help lighten us beyond our self-preoccupation with "me." Reflective walking is not only effective in working with loneliness; it can be used in processing any difficult emotion. It can also be an enjoyable way to simply be present while walking—anywhere, anytime.

The basic fear of aloneness may also include a related anxiety that is not usually recognized: the fear of disconnection—not only from others, but from our own heart. This sense of disconnection may be heightened as we age. It can penetrate deeper than loneliness and often manifests as a knotted quiver in the chest or abdomen. Remember, at its depths, the heart that seeks to experience our basic connectedness is more real than anything. It is the nameless drive that calls us to be who we most truly are. When we are not in touch with this, we may become caught in the existential anxiety of separation or disconnectedness.

Aging teaches us that eventually everyone will die. As people we know start to die, we become increasingly aware that we and our loved ones have limited time. Undoubtedly we will have times of feeling groundless and disconnected when this occurs. I remember that when I learned Elizabeth had breast cancer, I certainly felt the fear of disconnection and loss. But part of the wisdom of getting older comes when we're willing to acknowledge that these uncomfortable feelings are part of being human. The wisdom deepens when we breathe the aching fear of loss into the center of our chests and simply let it be there, no matter how uncomfortable we might feel.

When we stay really present with our discomfort, which may at times feel like a hole in the heart, it may open us to a basic understanding of the human condition—the realization that everyone suffers. When we can endure this existential space, and stay with it without answers and without pushing it away, it can become a doorway into what is most real. Resting in the heart, without trying to change anything, and surrendering to the reality of what life is—including but not limited to suffering—the experience can, mysteriously, transform into genuine equanimity.

Helplessness

While the experience of loneliness may be one of the most difficult trials of aging, encountering helplessness—where we feel powerless and a total loss of control—may be even more difficult. It is certainly something we're rarely prepared for, and helplessness can make even the strongest among us feel like a beginner.

When we are diagnosed with a serious illness, it is so easy to get on the positive-thinking bandwagon and declare that we're going to "win" this "battle with cancer" or other disease. When the reality of actually dealing with the symptoms, both physical and emotional, sets in, our outlook can rapidly change. The experience of helplessness may come as a shock, and it can quickly demoralize us. For example, when we are hospitalized, whether for surgery or for a serious condition, and are finally discharged, we may think that our crisis has been resolved. But nothing is the same. The numerous morbidities and uncertainties can make each day seem daunting. We may be challenged both physically and emotionally in ways that we couldn't have imagined. We may be shocked to find out how difficult it is to do simple physical therapy. It's not only exhausting; it can also be humiliating. The identity we had, as perhaps someone strong and self-reliant, is now challenged by a body that is frail and weak.

The frustrating cycle from remission and hope, and then

to the next flare-up and hopelessness, leaves our whole world unstable. Realizing that the end may be much closer than we previously anticipated, we may be tempted by the romantic notion to try to live each day as if it's our last. But the reality is we may have very little strength or energy to do the things we want, or even to "maintain a positive attitude." Traveling is often out of the question, and even eating out can become a struggle.

This is where we might face a crucial aspect of aging—being forced to look at what is really important to us. This might require honestly opening to our losses—especially the loss of the future we had imagined. This may bring us to tears, but we don't need to deny them. Being honest with ourselves and being open and vulnerable to those close to us are the kinds of things that make these difficult times also deeply worthwhile.

In my early forties I was diagnosed with a serious immune system disorder. For several years it was mostly in remission, but shortly after I turned forty-seven I experienced an acute and prolonged flare-up, with no indication that I would ever get better. For close to three years I watched my life as I had known it begin to fall apart. I lost my ability to work and engage in physical activities, as well as watching my basic identities be dismantled—being a seasoned meditator (and now unable to focus), being a carpenter and contractor (my livelihood), and being a husband and father. At first, it was disorienting and frightening not to have these props of self-identity. One day I took a shower and washed my hair, but it made me so exhausted I couldn't even step over the shower curb to dry myself. I was standing there feeling hopeless, with a sense of loss for which there seemed to be no remedy. At that time the feeling of helplessness was so strong that I didn't know where the courage to carry on would come from.

I remember one day going to the beach where I often used to jog and boogie board. This time I was standing on the boardwalk leaning against the railing, watching the surfers, the boogie boarders, the joggers, the teenagers playing football or throwing Frisbees—knowing I didn't have the strength to even walk down to the beach. It felt as if my life as I had known it was irretrievably lost, and it was very easy to fall into self-pity. Helplessness in itself is difficult enough, but when we add our emotions on top of it—self-pity, anger, anxiety—the helplessness feels even worse.

At the time I knew I needed help, but I didn't want to bother anyone. Elizabeth and I had been taking turns visiting each other—at the time she lived in San Diego and I lived in Northern California—but one time I asked her not to come. I just didn't want her to see me in such a weakened state. But that weekend someone knocked on my door, and when I opened it, to my great surprise she was standing there smiling. I remember how my pride dissolved in an instant, and how I saw through my pictures of how I was supposed to be—namely, strong and independent. My attempt to deny my dependence forced me to look at my attachment to my beliefs—especially about how things ought to be. It helped that Elizabeth didn't share these beliefs, and was able to extend herself regardless of whatever fears she may have been feeling about what might happen to me.

As I stayed with the fears—of helplessness, dependence, uncertainty—and particularly as I was able to bring the quality of compassion to the experience itself, there was a dramatic shift. As the illusory self-images were stripped away, I experienced the freedom of not *needing* to be anyone at all. By truly surrendering to the experience of helplessness, by letting everything I had been clinging to just fall apart, I found that what remained was more than enough. As we learn to breathe fear into the center of the chest, the heart feels more and more spacious. This heart is more spacious than the mind can ever imagine.

We all dread the helplessness of losing control; yet, real freedom lies in recognizing the futility of demanding that life be within our control. Instead, we must learn the willingness to feel—and to say Yes to—the experience of helplessness itself. This is one of the hidden gifts of serious illness or loss. It pushes us right to our edge, where we may have the good fortune to realize that our only real option is to surrender to our experience and let it just be.

One year Elizabeth and I took a trip to Barcelona. At the time I had an intestinal infection, including a fairly intense bout of diarrhea, but we decided to go anyway. Once we got to Barcelona, the diarrhea got worse, and even though I really should have stayed in the apartment we had rented, instead we took a train to visit a monastery. Halfway there I knew I had to get off the train to use the toilet, but when we entered the train station, it was mostly deserted and the bathrooms were locked. To my great humiliation I pooped in my pants—a literal example of the popular expression, "Shit happens." We had to walk several blocks to find a restaurant with a bathroom. To add to my humiliation the bathroom was out of toilet paper, but Elizabeth wasn't the least bit perturbed, and she proceeded to clean me up, with the many tissues in her bag. I had thought I could never go through something like that, but being helpless can be a great teacher. My only choice was to have the experience be exactly as it was, and to realize that my pride had to be surrendered. Once I was no longer identified with being strong and independent, instead of feeling horrible, we both were able to take the situation much more lightly, and the experience transformed from one of helplessness and powerlessness to one of genuine intimacy.

Another example: For years after I had surgery for cancer I had to deal with PTSD from the pain I experienced during some highly invasive procedures while I was in the hospital. For a long time I had to close my eyes when scenes from hospitals came on the TV. I just wanted to disappear when images of the painful procedures would pop back into my mind. As anyone with PTSD knows, the helplessness can easily turn into paralysis. In my case the helplessness was exacerbated by having to deal with the comorbidities, the medications, and the side effects of the medications—not knowing what to expect, not being able to plan beyond a few hours. It often left me with a vague sense of doom whenever I thought about the future. The loss of my physical strength intensified the feeling of powerlessness, and along with the doom I also experienced the world as a dangerous place—who knew what was coming next? This is a common experience for those dealing with similar circumstances where strongly believed fearful thoughts increase the experience of distress.

When I would get shooting pains through the nerves in my face and head, for instance, my mind would instantly return to the automatic thoughts: "Not again!" "Will it get worse?" "Will it ever stop?" "I can't take this!"

Yet, even when things seemed really bad, I still was able—although sometimes with difficulty—to remember to breathe into the chest center and cease resisting what is. When I remembered to do this, there was always a degree of equanimity. It wasn't that the pain or the anxiety disappeared, but there was a larger sense of Being, within which I knew, on some fundamental level, that I was okay.

Yet I'm also aware that things can change rapidly. I'm aware that for many people, the changes that come with aging, particularly around being and feeling helpless, can be objectively hard. By that I mean they are intrinsically difficult—not just because of our attitudes toward them or because we have the expectation that things should be otherwise. We can work with our attitudes and expectations; yet we can't deny the objective challenges that these situations present.

One challenge may arise when we have a long and increasingly debilitating illness. Over time we may discover that medical procedures and drugs are not always the best solution—in some cases the purely medical approach unequivocally decreases the quality of our life. At this point it will take courage to confront the realization that our life may be coming to an end. But it also takes courage to act on this, especially because it is often unclear what the best course of action may be. We have to be able to look clearly at our situation and the choices that are in front of us. When we have a serious or possibly terminal illness, we may fear making the mistake of prolonging our suffering with endless medical interventions. We may not want our remaining days to be controlled just by doctors and technology. On the other hand, we may also fear making the mistake of giving up on medical interventions too soon. It is important to be as prepared as we can before a critical decision is upon us. For this to happen we have to know what is most important to us. Do we want to keep trying the medical options even when there is very little quality of life, in the hope that things will turn around? Or do we want to devote the time we have left to family and the things and activities we value most? Once the tradeoffs are clear to us, we're more able to take the most beneficial actions.

When we face conditions in which there may be no clear path forward, sometimes people consider the possibility of consciously ending their life as an option. This is complicated, because unless one has a terminal illness and lives in a state where assisted suicide is legal, how one would end one's life needs to be carefully considered. In light of my own experience with periods which I felt were objectively hard, I've realized that there could be a time in the future, for some of us, where conscious suicide may be a possible option to consider. Although I don't feel that way now, I think it's important that anyone who is considering this possibility begin their preparations while they are still in good enough mental and physical shape to do so. Once dementia or the severe weakness of some other disability sets in, it may not be possible to have the clarity to make the necessary decisions and plans. Or to say goodbye in a way that would allow your loved ones to accept and be at peace with your decision.

Yet even when things are objectively hard, there is one meditation practice that I always find helpful. The purpose of this meditation is to move out of the very narrow focus on ourselves so that we can connect with the healing experience of tapping into the pain of others. Paradoxically, awareness of the suffering of others is often the exact antidote to our self-absorbed sense of hopelessness. Suffering is often the most effective vehicle for awakening the heart.

Compassion Meditation

To begin, first sit for a while, bringing attention to the center of the chest via the breath. Feel the texture, the quality, in the center of the chest.

Bring to mind your own physical/emotional distress. Feel it, as physically as possible, rather than focusing on the story line.

Then, bring to mind people who have the same or similar

difficulty you are dealing with, such as illness, fear, shame, etc. You can imagine the many people all over the world who share this pain, breathing this image into the heart on the in-breath. Then, on the out-breath, extend to them your wish that they be healed in their difficulties.

Feel the universality of the pain all people share. It's important to note that you are not taking on the burden of other people's pain; you are only bringing awareness to the fact that many people are suffering as you are.

Breathing them in again, include yourself and your own pain, and, on the out-breath, again extend the wish for healing—to the others, to oneself, to the pain we all share. Stay with this for a few breaths.

Staying with your distress, feel the sense of kinship with the other people in pain.

Feel the universality of the "shared being," the sense of connectedness with all people and life. This is the awakened heart that can encompass pain with compassion.

Even if you don't connect with the shared pain or the shared being, just come back to simply breathing in and out of the center of the chest for a few minutes. Feel the texture there.

Rest in the spaciousness of the heart.

Shorter Version

Here is a shorter version of the above meditation that can be used instantly anytime you are caught in a strong fear:

First, think of a friend who has a similar fear and extend kindness to this person by breathing him/her into the center of the chest on the in-breath. On the out-breath, say the line, "May you be healed in your difficulty."

Then, on the very next in-breath, breathe the sensations of your own fear into the center of the chest and, on the out-breath, extend kindness to yourself in the same way you did toward the friend.

For some reason, when we tap into the innate desire to wish another well, we can more easily channel that wish for well-being toward ourselves.

One other practice I use, as a shortcut to help me connect with a sense of compassion for others, as well as myself, is a short mantra: *"Everyone has pain. Everyone suffers. Everyone will die."* When I recite this, remembering its actual truth, it almost always serves as a reminder of a bigger sense of things, and often takes me out of my personal emotional distress.

No matter what practices we use, loneliness and helplessness may continue to be a challenge—yet living authentically as we age requires being open to change, to the unknown, to *whatever* arises. Yes, we fear change and discomfort, and we prefer the quiet waters, but in order to live more genuinely, we need to be wary that our desire for comfort and complacency are more pernicious than our fear of change. This whole process certainly takes courage; when we reach our lowest moments, a part of us gets exposed that we're rarely in touch with when things are going well. Yet when we enter into the depths of this consciously, it can open the door to inner freedom.

Surrendering to the physical reality of the present moment, we learn to go deeper with each in-breath. The experience of helplessness can transform even our worst fears into genuine equanimity, because it forces us to give up our deep attachments and surrender to what life is actually presenting.

8

Physical Pain

WHEN THE BUDDHA said that life is suffering, one of the things he surely had in mind was the inevitability of physical pain. After having surgery for kidney cancer several years ago, I had some serious post-surgical complications, and since then I've had to deal with chronic peripheral nerve pain. This was not my first experience of serious pain; I've had to work with pain and discomfort on and off for over thirty years—primarily from an immune system condition. And although I'm well aware that many people have much more pain than I do, this time the intensity of the pain got my attention in a way that forced me to reexamine the subtleties of working with physical pain.

I think it's accurate to say that when we have physical pain, we most often don't want to have much to do with it. Moreover, we seem to have the ability to quickly turn our physical pain into mental and emotional suffering.

The Pain Syndrome

When we experience physical pain, it is normal to have fear and concern. This is usually translated into an effort to make the pain go away. In fact, this is what we expect in our society—we often have the sense of entitlement that life *should* be free from pain. However, if our pain continues, one of the worst parts is the onset of the pain syndrome. Whether the pain is short term, like an injury, or long term, with chronic pain—in the pain syndrome our physical pain and our emotional reactions to it can become the primary focus of our attention. When this happens, our life begins to revolve almost completely around how we're feeling.

With chronic pain we may not know how long the pain will last, and when or if it will go away, and if it goes, we don't know when it will return. We can become constantly anxious that the pain will never stop, and when it stops, even though we may be glad that we are no longer in pain, we can become anxious in anticipating that it will begin again. What is happening is that our focus and personality begin to center more and more on our pain and its vicissitudes. This hypervigilance can also occur around illness. Even if an illness is successfully treated, we may fear that the cure will not last.

We may develop radar for any sign that the pain or illness is returning; any little pain or change in the body can bring on anxiety and even a feeling of doom. And often the suffering that we experience when this happens may actually be worse than the pain and illness itself. Considering that an estimated 100 million adults suffer from persistent or chronic pain in the United States alone, the need to find effective alternative ways to deal with pain as we age is enormous.

This doesn't mean we should never take medication. Sometimes, when pain is intense, alternative techniques may have to be supplemented with medications. With my own nerve pain, I've had to accept that at times I have to take medication. But once we start taking pain medication, we have to be wary of the potential downward spiral into dependency and addiction. It is a very delicate balancing act between taking the amount of pain medication necessary to bring relief, and avoiding the serious side effects that are always a danger when taking medication for pain. This is why it is helpful to find complementary therapies, such as acupuncture, yoga, and biofeedback—and the kinds of meditations and approaches to suffering I explore in this book.

Whatever we do, our approach needs to include awareness of how our emotion-based beliefs intensify the distress, and in remembering how to work with the pain, we may find the pain becomes a very powerful teacher.

Pain as Our Path to Awakening

When pain becomes chronic, it is natural that we will crave to be free from it. But when we place all of our attention on how to get rid of the pain, it is unlikely that our experience of pain will have any upside. Yet it's possible for both our pain and the suffering that arises from our pain, to become, in a way, our path, our teacher.

This happens when we discover that we can learn from them, and perhaps even experience our life more deeply and with more humility and appreciation. The understanding that pain can be our path to self-discovery is a fundamental change in how we relate to our experience; it allows us to begin to view and work with our pain, as well as our suffering, in a more conscious way. At the very least, we can view our pain as an opportunity to learn from our many attachments—especially from our attachment to comfort. There is also attachment to our body and to control. And in cases of chronic pain, there is also attachment to our future—the fear of what's going to happen to us. Yet, practicing with our pain is what allows us to gradually become free of these attachments, or at least to hold them more lightly.

When pain arises, instead of immediately thinking, "How can I get rid of this?" (motivated by my attachment to comfort)—I now ask, following Stephen Levine, "Here it is again, what will it be like this time?" From my own experience I know that it's not always easy to remember this, but when I do, it's like turning the whole experience right-side up. It's not that the pain necessarily goes away, but we're now relating *to* it rather than *from* it—less identified with the pain as who we are.

It's important to understand that in working with pain there is a difference between being cured and being healed. Saint Brigit, back in the seventh century, said that healing is always possible even when cure is unlikely. It's possible that we may never be cured of pain—in the sense that our pain will permanently go away. Yet we can still be healed—in the sense of becoming increasing free of our attachments.

We can feel the freedom that comes when we see through and drop our entitlement to comfort, or when we can refrain from indulging our anger or self-pity. Sometimes we may use our pain to make ourselves feel special—describing our plight to others so that we feel the subtle pleasure in playing the victim, singing our tune of "Woe is me." But if we can see through this and refrain from using our pain to make ourselves feel special, even if our pain remains, we are somewhat healed.

The obstacles to seeing pain as our path will vary, depending on the nature of our illness. My present experience with chronic nerve pain, which has been very persistent and often unabating for long periods, usually feels oppressive and sometimes overwhelming. To see it as my path requires constant mental reminders, because it is so easy to forget what "seeing it as my path" actually means.

I used to keep a cheat sheet with me wherever I went, using my own "Cliff's Notes" version of what I needed to do as a set of mental reminders to help me get through the most diffi-cult periods. (See the Cliff's Notes section at the end of this chapter.) Then, when the nerve pain began abating, there was a new challenge, because when the pain returned again, I was often surprised by it and almost always felt disappointment. It was amazing how, with each little remission, my expectations quickly reset to believe I was now and forever going to again be pain-free—an invitation to shock and disappointment.

But it's essential to understand that setbacks will most likely happen. When we understand this, we are less likely to be blindsided by them, and thus less likely to fall into a tailspin of discouragement and anxiety. *"Setbacks will happen!"* is a mantra that anyone with chronic pain should commit to memory. Now, no longer surprised with each new episode, I have learned to remember to pause, take a breath into the heart, say "Hello" to the pain, and then greet it with curiosity.

Once we remember to treat pain with curiosity, the one essential thing to recognize is that pain is one thing and how we relate to it is another. Often they get intermingled into one confused whole, rather than our realizing that pain is the phys-ical experience of discomfort and how we relate to it is more mental and emotional.

We may tend to relate to pain from the emotion of fear or self-pity, and this makes the experience of pain more intense. The alternative is to begin to relate to pain with an element of curiosity—being willing to relax into it and explore it—where the experience of pain is usually more tolerable.

Pain, Suffering, and the Need for Distractions

And yet—it's important to recognize that there may be times when nothing we do will give us much relief, either from the physical pain or the suffering that arises from it. Truthfully, there are times when my only response to the recurring experience of pain may be, "Oh, shit!" At those times, intentionally and consciously doing things to distract us from our bodies and minds is sometimes a healthy thing to do. This should certainly include doing things we genuinely have enjoyed doing, like, for me, walking in nature or listening to my favorite music.

I even made a list of the things I most love to do, since it's so easy, when in pain, or when depressed or disheartened, to forget about the things that can bring us joy. One thing that always helps me is taking a walk outside with my headset on, listening to oldies from the sixties and singing along out loud. It's like good food for our Being. We can also include activities that simply distract us, like watching TV or reading—anything we can use to forget ourselves, at least temporarily. If it is done consciously, rather than unconsciously, which is what we usually do, it can be like a pause in time to refresh us—allowing us to return to being present with our difficulties as soon as we are able. This is a way of being gentle and kind to ourselves and our situation. It is also a way of bringing a semblance of control to our difficult situation, and many have found that taking an active role in dealing with their pain is actually healing, in that it keeps us from spinning downward into cycles of powerlessness and hopelessness.

We also need to be aware of the tendency to isolate when we're in pain. We may isolate because we think that others can't possibly understand what we're going through, or we don't want to burden them. We may even feel guilty. But these thoughts, along with feeling isolated and cut off from friends, just make our experience of pain more intense. One thing I've found is that, despite whatever hesitancy I had, it has always been helpful to talk to a friend—to honestly share what I am thinking and feeling. This isn't about looking for advice or expecting the other person to take away my pain; it's a reminder never to underestimate the value of genuine human connection. If we don't feel we have anyone we can truly talk to, it may take an effort on our part to reach out. But it's an effort that's well worth taking—feeling isolated only increases our suffering.

Pain and Mental Suffering

Even though practicing with physical pain can sometimes be very difficult, the truth is, it's nonetheless often workable and even potentially worthwhile.

Even more, we can discover that it's possible to significantly reduce the suffering that arises out of our physical pain, for example, the suffering that's generated from negative judgments like, "Why is this happening to me?" or "I can't bear this" or "Poor me." First we need to recognize these judgments *as* judgments, as a filter that we add on. And we also need to see how we normally accept them, unquestioned, as the truth. This recognition will allow us to see how the blind belief in our thoughts solidifies our physical experience of pain into the heaviness of suffering, as well as increasing the physical pain by causing the body to constrict.

One of the thoughts that anyone who experiences chronic illness or pain will have to deal with is the thought that we want our old life back. We feel grief for the body we no longer have, and our thoughts tend to reinforce the denial that this is, in fact, our life. Yet, with each thought where we lament what we no longer have, we are wasting the precious energy that we need to focus on how to best deal with the life we actually have now.

Another pernicious and very common tendency of the thinking mind is catastrophizing—where we automatically exaggerate and magnify the threat of pain and anticipate the worst. When we get trapped in this way of thinking, the whole experience can seem overwhelming. This is where we can tell ourselves, "Not happening now!"—a helpful reminder that we don't actually have a medical diagnosis right now. Or, even if we have a diagnosis, imagining the worst future scenarios just makes things much worse. Using this phrase allows us to uncover how much mental spinning we're adding, and how it obscures the reality of the present moment. This phrase is a reminder that most of what is causing us anxiety in the present moment is only happening in our mind.

When we say "Not happening now!" we can follow it by asking, "What am I adding?" This question points us directly to thoughts such as "I can't do this," which is based on a negative self-image of being incapable. We also have to be careful about adding self-judgments, such as, "This pain is my fault because I can't handle stress," or "This pain proves that I'm bad." Judgments like these certainly aren't logical, but that carries little weight when we're stuck in believing them. We suffer even more when we add the deep-seated belief that life *should* be free from pain—"I shouldn't have to go through this!"—which is rooted in the sense of entitlement we all have to some degree. In resisting our pain by holding on to this entitlement, we strengthen the very pain that we're trying to avoid.

In each of these examples we're adding a mental spin to what is happening. In fact, in many examples of our emotional distress, what we're adding to the present moment is something either from the past or from an imagined future, and in each case it makes the situation worse. "Not happening now!" has become one of my favorite phrases, primarily because it is so direct; it cuts right through our tendency to catastrophize. It's like poking a pin in a balloon, in that our distress often quickly disappears.

Along with catastrophizing, another pernicious mental tendency is negative filtering, where we ignore all of our positive experience and magnify the negative aspects. When we focus on our pain, we're often ignoring the people and things we care about and not appreciating the numerous things that are right in front of us.

Objectifying Beliefs

Recognizing our pain-related beliefs with precision is the first step in loosening their hold on us. Once they're recognized, we can begin to objectify them, by naming or labeling them, and even writing them down.

For example, identifying and naming thoughts like, "I can't take this," "What's going to happen to me?" and "Why me?" is especially helpful in letting us step outside of them. Unless we name or label them as mere thoughts, we will most likely see ourselves as a victim of our pain. However, with the objective awareness that comes with labeling them, such thoughts can eventually be seen as thoughts and nothing more. In fact, we can begin to realize that they may not even be true! And, as a consequence, we can feel a little more space around the actual pain, so we're less caught in it.

When we have a strong thought, like "This is too much" or "Poor me," there is almost always a deep-seated fear right underneath the thought. The fear is there, lurking, but often not recognized. Sometimes it's helpful to ask ourselves, "What specifically am I afraid of?" We may find that the driving fear is of danger—perhaps of having to deal with increasing pain. Or we may have the fear of loss of control that comes when we worry that the pain may never end. One thing is certain: learning to work with our pain is much more difficult when we're caught in fear, and part of the art of being with pain requires that we first learn to open to our fears. Normally we try to shut them out, but what if we could instead learn not to fight them? As Ram Dass says, invite them in for a cup of tea. The idea is to learn to turn our dread into curiosity.

As we've seen, curiosity means that we're willing to explore unknown territory—the places where the protective ego doesn't want to go. Curiosity allows us to take a step at our edge, delving into the hidden corners of our unwanted fears. Bringing curiosity allows a kind of spaciousness to envelop even our most difficult experiences. We are no longer so caught up in the dark and grim story of "me and my pain," but more able to relate to the difficulty from a larger sense of things. This spaciousness lets us feel a little sense of lightness even in the midst of our pain—a lightness that comes from willingly opening to our pain and our fears with curiosity.

Part of our difficulty with pain, and the suffering that arises out of it, comes from the language we use to talk about it. Since our choice of words can shape how we perceive and react to reality, it's sometimes helpful to use different language when dealing with pain. For example, when we think of pain in terms of the enemy and resist even a hint of it, we automatically make the pain stronger. That is one reason why using the language that pain is the path, rather than the enemy, is an important step in dealing with pain.

Here's another example of using different language: instead

of saying, "I'm in pain"—where we are totally identified with the pain ("my pain is me"), including the unspoken connotation of gloom and doom—we can simply say, "There is pain here." Saying "There is pain here" immediately allows us to step back from our identification with the pain and gives us some mental space around the situation. However, as helpful as this may be, to truly work with physical pain requires more than just a change in language.

Working with Pain Directly

One effective way of working with the physical experience of pain itself is to focus on the specific physical sensations of the pain directly. We can do this by using the breath to breathe into the pain and then staying with the breath/pain as we breathe in and out.

Working with Pain

Using the breath to breathe into the pain, bring awareness to wherever you're experiencing tightness or a pushing away— gently softening into these painful areas with the light touch of awareness.

We can then ask a series of questions to the pain:

- Can you simply say "Hello" to it—welcoming it with curiosity?
- If you can't welcome it, can you say "Hello" to the resistance?
- Where specifically is the pain located in the body?
- Is it on the surface or is it deeper? Specifically, how deep?

- What does the strongest sensation actually feel like? Feel it.
- Can you breathe into it? Soften into it?
- How big is it? What shape is it?
- What word would best describe its texture—aching, stabbing, sharp, or burning?
- Is there a pressure or throbbing?
- How intense is it, on a scale from 1 to 10?
- What is its color?
- Again, can you breathe into the physical sensations and feel them?
- Are there any strong thoughts associated with the sensations?
- What word would describe the emotional quality, like anger, or anxiety, or sadness?
- Can you say "Hello" to the emotional feeling in the body?

It's often helpful to repeat this series of questions one or two more times and see how the answers change.

In asking such questions, which is the essence of curiosity, we will find that we can be much more precise in experiencing what we're feeling. We may also find that with each question we become a little less identified with the pain—experiencing it from the "witness." This is a way of approaching the pain with the curiosity of a scientist—relating *to* it rather than *from* it. When we relate from our pain, we stay in a subjective narrow bubble that only magnifies the pain. But when we relate *to* it, from outside of it, the experience of pain can be significantly softened. This allows us to experience the pain, at least some of the time, as just strong sensations. Focusing on it intently, even if it feels like white heat, it will no longer feel quite so "painful." In fact, the sensations often change fairly rapidly—from throbbing to aching to dull—sometimes even disappearing. This can take us out of the catastrophic thinking that tells us that our pain will *always* be horrible or unbearable.

Watching this whole process with curiosity is key.

Opening into Awareness

Another effective way to work with pain is to intentionally focus on the breath itself. Normally, when we're in pain, the painful sensations fill up the entire awareness channel connected to the brain. Picture a conduit that sends the pain signals to the brain, and picture the conduit completely filled with the painful signals. But when we include a focused attention to the breath—which may require our full concentration—the pain only fills up part of the awareness channel, since awareness is so attuned to the breath. This allows the pain to be experienced differently, within a larger container of awareness. Focusing on the breath is even more effective when we take the longer and slower breaths associated with deep relaxation. As the body relaxes, the intensity of physical pain will often lessen.

Additionally, when in substantial pain, an expanded version of focusing on the breath is to ask, "And?" This reminds us to ask *where else* we can direct our awareness, other than obsessively fixating on the pain. We can look to some other aspect of the present moment, such as sounds. We can ask "And?" again and become aware of the air, or the temperature, or the sense of space. This practice helps us remember to let awareness open to the full experience of the present moment. Opening to the present moment is a teaching that is emphasized repeatedly in many spiritual traditions, but the truth is, to really pay attention to the totality of our experience is a rare occurrence; it is something that has to be consciously cultivated. Asking "And?" allows us to expand awareness beyond just our physical symptoms of pain, and in this sense the pain actually pushes us to do exactly what we aspire to do—be more awake and present.

When we feel the pain of a headache or stomachache, for instance, we first consciously feel it, but then also feel the breath. *And*, we hear the sounds. *And*, we look at what is in front of us—and on and on. The effort is soft, that is, without strain. And as awareness expands to include these other sensations and perceptions, we feel the edges of the pain soften and begin to blend into the wider awareness—the pain becoming less and less solid as we experience it melt into awareness itself. In this way the pain no longer fills up our awareness—it becomes simply another sensation. And by being fully present with the whole of our experience we can avoid the downward spiral into anxiety and depression that often accompanies chronic pain.

Sometimes, with practice, we can let ourselves feel our pain fully, and then the pain is not so bad. It is there, but it feels controllable. Sometimes we can even feel a degree of equanimity. But sometimes, regardless of our practice, pain can be beyond agony, or at least beyond our ability to be present to it. Be kind to yourself: to want the pain to go away does not mean we are a spiritual failure—it simply means we're human.

Again, some pain can be beyond what we can tolerate, and some chronic pain—which keeps coming and coming with no hope of relief—can overwhelm even the strongest spiritual practitioner. When this happens, it's helpful to remember that sometimes things are just objectively hard, and our usual practice efforts may have little effect. It doesn't mean spiritual practice doesn't work, or that we're bad practitioners, or that we should give up—thoughts that can easily lead to a sense of defeat and despair. We just have to learn that in instances like these we have to do whatever we can to ride them out, including finding whatever distraction or comfort that might work, even if only for a temporary respite.

Yet, if nothing else, these instances where the pain is beyond tolerable can teach us humility—in that we are not special, we are not in control, and we can't overcome everything through effort.

Bringing Kindness to Our Pain

We can also use the breath to gently touch into the pain— breathing into the physical sensations almost as if the breath were giving a gentle massage to the pain. This is especially helpful with long-term or chronic pain.

I sometimes have periods of nausea, a symptom of the immune system disorder I've had for many years. When the nausea is intense, I often have to curl up into a fetal position in bed, and my practice is to breathe into the center of the chest on the in-breath and then extend kindness or healing energy to my body, to my immune system, via the out-breath—just as you would extend compassion to someone you cared about who was in distress. Extending kindness or healing to oneself isn't a mental exercise—it is an energetic response that we can actually feel in the body. Sometimes I put one hand on the center of my chest, and the other hand on the area where the discomfort is located. The act of touch seems to subtly add the sense of warmth to the overall experience. The point isn't to make the nausea go away, but to relate to it in a friendlier way.

When I touch into the nausea, I wordlessly say "Hello" to it, and remind it that it's not the enemy. With the increasing sense of spaciousness and heart that comes from practicing in this way, I have found I can gradually stay with the sensations of nausea for quite some time. And in the moments when I can experience the nausea not as "pain," but as just intense physical energy, I'm sometimes struck by a sense of quiet joy, where it is clear that who we truly are is so much more than just this body.

It is also clear that, contrary to what most people believe, it is certainly possible to feel equanimity even while in discomfort.

Moreover, we may discover that our physical pain is not personal—which is to say it is not somehow directed at us, as it may sometimes seem. When we get angry with our physical pain and ask, "Why me?" we are often taking it personally. But in fact our physical pain is just the result of an agitation of our nerve endings. It is the body doing what bodies do: they slowly deteriorate, break down, and malfunction—whether from an external cause, such as an accident, or through our normal internal process of aging.

To accept our pain is to understand this—that this is part of the natural order of things. But accepting our pain is not the same as resignation—which implies a passive giving up. It's more a case of having it be the way it is. Accepting pain as part of one's life takes courage, and it is anything but passive. Part of accepting our pain is learning to take it less personally, thus giving it less power over us.

Using Pain to Go Deeper

To refrain from being caught up in our reactions to pain may require having a bigger sense of purpose. Nietzsche once said that "one who has a *why* to live for can bear almost any *how*." In

other words, a sense of purpose can help us withstand whatever seeming obstructions may arise. For me, the "why"—the
purpose—is to use the physical pain as an entry into the Heart.
Pain that is chronic and fairly constant, like nerve pain, can be
used as a doorway to going deeper into the heart of awareness.
When I become aware of the nerve pain, I use it as a reminder
to breathe deeply into the center of the chest on the in-breath,
and on the out-breath to simply rest in awareness. Sometimes
I silently say:

> Breathing in, dwelling in the Heart;
> Breathing out, just Being.

Each in-breath goes deeper into the heart; each out-breath
puts me more in contact with a deeper awareness.

When I remember to use my pain to go deeper into the
Heart, I can sometimes experience a larger sense of myself
and of life. Residing in the Heart essentially means we're no
longer caught in the head, in all of our self-centered thoughts,
judgments, and expectations. Most importantly, we no longer
identify with our pain as who we are or the focal point of life,
but rather we identify with a vaster, more heartfelt sense of
what life is. Regardless of what we might be feeling physically
or emotionally, we understand that we are not limited or defined
by those feelings. Sometimes this allows us to experience an
equanimity that is beyond our conceptual understanding.

We can have a bigger sense of purpose even in those moments
when pain seems to be getting the best of us. Sometimes we
can remember to say "Yes" to the pain, which means, instead
of saying, "No, not again," or, "I can't stand this," we're willing to actually feel what's there. Sometimes I even say, "Do
your worst, pain!" This is not said with grim determination or

as an angry defiance; it is actually a lighthearted attitude that helps me to avoid falling into feeling like a victim. It's no longer fighting what feels like the enemy; rather it's a back-and-forth engagement that feels more poignant than like a struggle. In fact, sometimes it even feels a little playful.

At other times, when pain arises, I also say "So what!"—a message to myself that this isn't the big deal my mind wants to make it. It's just my body doing its thing. I have to be careful to do this gently—not being willful in trying to overcome the pain. Being gentle and open to actually feeling what's present is the key to letting pain become the teacher—to letting the pain take us deeper into our experience, which is no longer just the painful sensations, but a more conscious experience of the moment. This engagement—this willingness to say Yes to the pain—definitely takes courage, because it means we are not going to turn away from the unpleasant. It may indeed be frightening at times to open to our pain, particularly when it's a brand-new pain, beyond what we've already experienced. We may fear that it will overcome us. In this case working with the fear may be just as important as working with the pain itself. But however we approach it, we are using the unpleasantness to break free of our sense of entitlement to comfort.

The Emergence of Compassion

One other form of learning that comes from practicing with our pain is the increased awareness of other people who also may be suffering. Most of the time we can conveniently turn away from the suffering of others, but when we're in pain, our normal ways of protecting ourselves tend to fall away. Our sense of entitlement, our sense of being special, no longer carries much weight. Regardless of our wealth or education, or whatever we hold on to to insulate ourselves from the plight of others, we can no longer deny that we are all equals. Pain is the great equalizer—it humbles us into the realization that we're all in this life together.

One practice I do when I'm having bouts of strong physical pain is the same as the practice I recommend for working with loneliness and helplessness. I picture people I know who are also in pain, and then I remember the countless others I don't know who are also in pain in that very moment. Then, on the in-breath, I breathe the images of those in pain into the center of the chest, and, on the out-breath, extend the wish for healing—to myself as well as to all the others. This practice is presented in the form of a meditation in the prior chapter on Loneliness and Helplessness.

In this way, our personal pain connects us with the pain of others—the pain we all share in various forms. This can deepen our sense of compassion and the wish that the suffering of others be healed. It will also diminish the sense of isolation we often feel when we're in pain.

When discouraged or feeling isolated, we can deepen our compassion further by actually doing something—even a little thing—to give ourselves to another. We can call up someone we know who is hurting. Or we can make ourselves available to someone even if we're not feeling well. Along with whatever help we might be extending this also takes our attention off of ourselves, which in itself can bring some relief. Helping others, even in little ways, also is one of the most effective ways of experiencing our basic connectedness, and is almost always satisfying. However, we need to be careful not to extend help with the expectation of *getting appreciation* in return. Giving just to get is neither helpful nor satisfying. It's also important to avoid falling into the role of a martyr—seeing ourselves as a suffering soul who still gives to others despite our own suffering. Self-awareness is essential to avoid falling into whatever detours are part of the terrain of offering compassion.

What makes it most difficult to experience compassion is remaining stuck in a self-centered stance toward life—a stance which is so easily reinforced when we are feeling pain. In fact, as I mentioned earlier, one of the qualities of pain that makes it so difficult is that it tends to fill up all of our mental space, to the extent that our lives end up revolving almost completely around how we're feeling, both physically and emotionally. But when we can intentionally bring awareness to the breath, as well as bringing to mind the suffering of others in pain, the pain no longer takes up all the space. As a consequence, we can feel it and even learn from it. The mantra I use to remind me of this is three simple phrases: "Everyone has pain. Everyone suffers. Everyone will die." It is especially helpful to remember these lines when I have a negative judgment about someone. When I remember to say these words, it doesn't take long for the judgment to fall away.

Learning from Pain

A while back a doctor told me to take a particular medication for nausea. I took it and it worked like a miracle. But what I realized was that if I had known about this pill for the prior thirty years since my nausea began, I never would have learned how to work with it, nor gone nearly as deeply into seeing my discomfort as a path to being more awake. Nor would I have been able to experience the depth of appreciation for life or the compassion for others that I often feel, even while still lying in bed in a fetal position. However, as I've said, there are times when our physical pain may leave us little choice but to take medication.

There will no doubt also be times when we may feel psychologically over our heads in dealing with physical discomfort. The experience of powerlessness that sometimes arises can wrap itself tightly around our small sense of self and cover us with what feels like a cloak of doom. Here too, when feeling this sense of gloom or doom, it is valuable to bring awareness to the center of the chest, breathing as if we were breathing the dark feelings directly into the chest center. With each breath you breathe the feelings in a little deeper. And with a long slow exhale you just exhale, not trying to change or let go of anything, but rather simply feeling what's there.

It may be that breathing into the chest center triggers the parasympathetic response of calm, which produces the endorphins that naturally reduce pain—but it's more than that. Who really knows what actually happens during this process of breathing into the chest center? Ultimately, it's a mystery. Nonetheless, you can experience for yourself how this practice allows us to gently experience what at times would otherwise feel unbearable. Surrendering to our deep fear of groundlessness can sometimes put us in touch with the fundamental awareness of just Being—the true ground that is always available to us.

Even if we don't have intense pain, it is well worth the effort to work with our small pains now. If it is our destiny as we age to have to deal with more intense pain down the road, this makes it possible not to be blindsided by it or have to start from square one. At the very least, try to remember that even though we may not want pain, it can at times push us toward inner freedom in ways we would never push ourselves on our own.

Part of what I've learned in working with physical pain is that really being with one's life *as it is* means no longer longing for the past. This requires being able to acknowledge and process one's losses, such as loss of physical abilities and good health. It also means not living in expectations of the future—either the assumption that things will automatically be better or that they will be worse. But to do this requires being able to acknowledge and surrender to uncertainty, because sometimes things change rapidly, with little or no warning, and we are left with the uncomfortable realization that we don't really know what will happen in the future.

This is why one of the most important teachings is to simply persevere with the practice, even when our mood becomes fearful and dark. Simply to remember to stay with the breath and not let our negative thoughts take over is a crucial step. And if we can add to that the quality of kindness—where we extend to ourselves the same compassion that we would to someone we cared about who was in a similar situation—we have the chance of not getting caught in the downward spiral that often takes over when we have pain. Even when pain becomes chronic, we can still remember not to allow it to become the primary focus of our attention, and instead be sure that we continue to do the things that we love.

We may find that our pain can push us into a deeper and ultimately more appreciative experience of what it means to be genuinely alive.

Pain Meditation

The following meditation is meant to be read slowly, leaving time for the meaning of each line to sink in. It can be read to oneself, or, if we are unable, it can be read to us by someone else. Even if we can't relate to every line, there are bound to be certain lines or phrases that will help remind us that our pain does not have to defeat us. Even more, the words can help us use the pain to have a deeper and more genuine experience of what our life is.

Take whatever position is comfortable, including lying down. As much as is possible, try to stay still.

Take a couple of deeper breaths to relax into the body. Notice where there is pain or discomfort, and allow your awareness to gently approach that area.

Use each arising of pain as a reminder of your wish to become inwardly free. Recall that each arising of pain can help you work with your attachment to comfort, to the body, and to control.

As you begin to approach the pain, say "Hello" to it—greeting the feelings of pain as just sensations, not as the enemy that must be overcome.

If there is resistance, say "Hello" to the resistance itself. Soften around the edges of the pain, until you can gently touch it with awareness.

Approaching the pain directly, notice specifically where it is located. As you softly breathe into it, notice how big it is.

As you breathe into it again, notice its shape.

Going deeper into the pain, feel its texture.

Is it hard or soft? Rough or smooth? Notice if it feels warm or cool.

Is there a pressure or throbbing? Do the sensations of discomfort move or stay still?

As awareness gently touches the pain, can you feel the sensations soften and lighten?

Focusing on the quality of the sensations of pain, see the difference between the sensations and your reactions to them.

Hear the mind's voice that says such things as "Poor me," "Why is this happening to me?" "What's going to happen to me?" Separating the thoughts from the sensations, notice how the pain lessens in intensity.

Continue breathing into the pain, again saying "Hello" to it, not letting the catastrophic thoughts get traction. The thoughts, based in fear, only solidify the pain.

Separating from them, you can feel the pain without fear. You can feel the pain as just sensations in the body.

As you feel the texture of the pain, also bring awareness to the quality of the breath. Feel the breath as distinct from the pain.

Let awareness expand to take in the breath along with the pain.

While staying with the breath and the pain, expand awareness again to include the environment.

Feel the air around you. Notice the quality of light. Hear the ambient sounds. Stay with the pain, but within the expanded container of breath and environment.

Notice how the edges of the pain soften and blend into awareness itself.

Notice the size of the pain and see if it's different from before.

Saying "Hello" to the pain, it is no longer the enemy.

To extend kindness to the pain, follow the in-breath to the center of the chest, and on the out-breath, send the wish for healing to the pain, using the exhale to massage the area of discomfort—not trying to get rid of the pain, but extending kindness to ourselves exactly as we are.

Wish yourself well as we would any friend in need.

Alternating breathing into the pain, including awareness of the breath and the environment, and extending kindness into the pain, allow the mind to increasingly relax into awareness itself—no longer just the body in pain.

Resting in awareness, touch the reality of just Being.

Bring to mind others you know who are also in pain. Picture each one struggling in their difficulty.

Now try to picture the many unknown others in the same or similar pain to your own.

Breathe the images of the others in pain into the center of the chest, and on the out-breath extend the wish for all that they be healed in their difficulties.

Breathing them in again, include yourself.

On the out-breath, again extend the wish for healing—to others, to oneself, to the pain we all share.

No longer just a body in pain.

Let each arising of pain invite you to dwell in the Heart.

No longer just a body in pain.

Rest in awareness itself.

There's a lot of information in this chapter, as well as many practical suggestions. If you're suffering from physical pain, especially chronic pain, I suggest you reread this entire chapter at least a few times and do the meditation as often as you are able.

I myself reread this chapter several times since I originally wrote it, and I always find something useful that I've forgotten, or I'm able to see things on a little deeper level.

We should never forget that we're all beginners.

However bad things may be for you, I'm confident that this material can help in your healing.

Cliff's Notes on Working with Pain

The following questions can be reminders of some of the techniques in this chapter. It might be helpful to carry a copy of these questions with you, and instead of being blindsided when pain arises, you can choose which questions and techniques might be most helpful.

Cliff's Notes on Physical Pain

1. Can I see this pain as my path—to free my attachment to comfort, the body, and control?
2. Can I remember that pain is one thing and how I relate to it is another?
3. Can I recognize and refrain from catastrophizing, and from adding emotional reactions, entitlements, negative thoughts?
4. When pain arises, instead of saying, "I'm in pain," can I simply say, "There is pain now"?
5. Instead of "Oh no!" can I say "Hello" to the pain, and ask, with genuine curiosity, "What will it be like this time?"
6. Can I breathe into the sensations directly, asking focused questions on size, shape, texture, etc.?
7. Can I remember to include awareness of breath and environment—putting space around the pain?
8. Can I breathe into the chest center, extending kindness to myself and to the pain on the out-breath?
9. Each time pain arises, can I remember to breathe deeply into the Heart, resting in awareness itself?
10. Can I challenge my fear of pain and embrace the whole experience, lightly saying, "Do your worst, pain!"?

11. Can I include others who are also in pain, and extend the wish for healing to them as well as to myself?
12. If necessary, can I find conscious distractions, especially the things that I truly enjoy?

PART III

Renewal

9

The Search for Meaning

As we age, we may experience periods when life seems aimless or lacks a sense of meaning. This can even happen when we're young, when we can sometimes live mindlessly, day to day, or just for sensual pleasure and enjoyment. As we get a little older, we may live with more of a sense of purpose, perhaps to be more productive or to acquire, which can make our lives feel more solid. But as we reach retirement or no longer have a role as a productive or important person, we may begin to feel obsolete.

This can become even more acute as we become less physically able and lose some of the identities we have had—like being athletic, or conventionally attractive, or self-sufficient. When this happens, we may feel that our lives no longer matter. We may even feel like we're a burden to others, and we may find ourselves with a lingering sense of insignificance and meaninglessness. Some may believe that they're just surviving—with the main motivation being just to get through the day. But even if we stay active and engaged, it's not unusual as we get older to look back on our lives and feel a sense of regret for the things we haven't done, or even feel that in some way we've been a failure. Some may even feel that they have never lived "their real life"—the life they believe they were "meant" to live.

Those who consider themselves spiritual sometimes focus on wanting to have a "good death," perhaps equating a good death—meaning one with equanimity—with proof that their life was worthwhile. Ultimately though, how we die may be totally beyond our control. What we may be missing is the fact that it's *how we live* that is much more important than whether or not we have a "good death."

For some, how we live, at any age, is something that often seems to be still somewhat within our control. To that extent, we may not be challenged by things that disturb our sense of meaning. Also, at any age, we can experience the meaningfulness of living a life devoted to self-discovery. Or, we may live to create, to serve, to love. The point is: our sense of meaning has little to do with how *long* we live or our moment of death, but rather with whether the way we live is aligned with our values.

Maybe you're not particularly worried about death, but perhaps you've still had periods when you questioned whether there was any enduring meaning in life. Maybe you asked the question "Is this all there is?" or "What is the point?" This isn't unusual, since by nature we seem to be programmed to seek meaning. In fact, it's said that humans are biologically wired in such a way that our brains automatically try to organize our experience into ordered patterns. So from the point of view of survival, it makes perfect sense that our minds would instinctively search for meaning and structure, to give us a sense of control in the face of a world that might otherwise appear dangerous or chaotic.

Reinterpreting the apparent chaos of life is often one of the prime functions of religion. In this sense, religion can make us feel a part of something bigger and provide meaning. It may provide an inspiring narrative to make sense of things and enable us to deal with the difficulties that we face in life, especially things like uncertainty and death. Religion can provide a context, or an overview, in which suffering makes sense, rather than being disheartening.

But as useful as such a view may be, we must remember that any philosophical or religious explanation is somewhat arbitrary. In fact, it is not even an explanation; it is more a description—and only one of many possible descriptions. This is why we need to beware of falling into the false comfort of seeing religious or spiritual teachings as the objective truth—or seeing our own religion as the only, or the best, teaching.

The truth is subtle, complex, and paradoxical; it is a mystery, and thus it is basically unknowable through the conceptual mind. Yet, it's easy to get attached to so-called spiritual truths and forget that, ultimately, we don't really know. We can talk about enlightenment, for instance, and reduce it to some solid picture of what enlightenment is, but in so doing we couldn't be further from the mystery of things.

It's pretty much a given that we will try to figure out what life is. We will say that life is difficult, or that life is an adventure or an opportunity. We might say that life is a gift or, as I just have, a mystery. But all of these are just descriptive stories—life can't be accurately summed up so simply with just a few words. You could even say that life isn't anything—but even that isn't saying anything!

We can search for meaning and then do our best to live from that—yet even so it's important to keep in mind that the meaning we posit is not an absolute reality. Rather, it is a practical response—a way to help us address the groundlessness we feel when the world seems to have no inherent meaning. This, as one thinker put it, is the existential dilemma: that we are beings who search for meaning and certainty in a universe that may very well have neither.

Yet, the question of meaning can be a compelling motivator. When we feel a loss of direction or little sense of purpose or feel obsolete, as if our lives don't seem to really matter, we may first use the usual props—such as busyness, entertainments, distractions, and even relationships—to cover over the feeling of emptiness inside. Then when these props don't work, we may seek spiritual answers to address the dilemma of an inner aimlessness in our lives.

When we feel helpless and anxious about the inner sense of chaos, we naturally want to find answers as a way to feel some sense of comfort and control. Yet, in trying to find the answer to the meaning of life, we may time and again experience frustration, because any conceptual answer we come up with will fall short in the face of the realities of life, especially the difficulties we face as we age. And at some point we may realize that we'll never find a satisfying answer through thinking alone.

At such times, we may seek the guidance of others who have also struggled with these questions. But we don't just want an intellectual answer to the meaning of life; we also want to know what we need to do in order to actually experience the clarity and satisfaction of a meaningful existence. Yet it's unrealistic to expect that someone can answer these questions for us: haven't we sometimes believed something we've been told, only to be disillusioned later? At best, we may be told that the answer we're looking for can only be found in how we live our lives. This means that rather than simply believing what we're told, a more grounded approach is to get out of our heads and instead enter fully into our lived experience.

In doing so, we may discover what others have—*that there is a definitive and visceral taste of meaning that comes with being present and engaged with whatever our life is at a given moment.* This experience does not need an intellectual justification; it is justifying in and of itself. However, we have to experiment with this in order to confirm it for ourselves.

Here's what it comes down to: we are wired to live, not just to think, and we need to engage in meaningful activity for the question of meaning to no longer matter.

When I first started thinking about writing this book, I believed I was not yet ready. Although I knew that I had something to say, the fact was I felt I didn't yet have enough of a clear overview to write something worthwhile. Whenever I would think about writing, I experienced a degree of anxiety and confusion, based on a sense of lack of purpose. But instead of trying to figure out what I might want to say, my practice was to try to stay present with what was actually happening, which was the anxiety and confusion itself. After a time, the anxiety and confusion completely disappeared, and it became clear to me that I was more than ready to begin. And as soon as I began writing, I experienced the deep satisfaction of doing something that felt truly meaningful. Staying present with the doubt and anxiety, combined with the activity of engaging in my writing, answered the questions that my mind could never have addressed satisfactorily. In fact, it made the questions irrelevant.

The question of meaning, from one point of view, can be met like a Zen koan, where the practice is to sit and be present with the question itself. The real question, and perhaps the most effective approach in our search for meaning, is to ask of life: *"What is this?"*

This, in essence, is what I was asking when I was debating whether to start writing this book. I was directly questioning my experience of doubt and confusion. This question is not an analytical question, in that it does not require an intellectual or factual answer. In fact, the question "What is this?" is asking us to bypass our tendency to try to understand things with the mind.

So how do we answer without using the mind in the usual

way? We do it by bringing a focused attention to the physical reality of our present moment experience. For example, right now, ask yourself the question, "What is this?"

The "this" is whatever you are experiencing right now.

"What Is This?" Meditation

Start by finding and focusing in on the strongest sensation in the body.

Now add awareness of the breath, and breathe into the strongest body sensations.

What does it really feel like to breathe into the body?

Stay with this for a few breaths, occasionally repeating the question "What is this?" silently to yourself—and taking care not to let the mind's speculations take over. Remember to put them on "call waiting" again and again.

Now ask the question again, and this time expand the attention to include the entire body—the sense of energy in the body, the whole of your physical self.

The effort is still focused, but instead of a narrow experience on just one small part of the present moment, there is a more expanded focus.

Keep asking "What is this?" as you stay with this expanded experience of the present moment.

Now expand the awareness one more time. Let the effort soften and widen so you can experience the whole or gestalt experience of simply sitting there, essentially not doing anything other than being aware.

In asking, "What is this?" you may still have awareness of the breath and body, but the answer now includes the experience of just Being.

Just observing and feeling—resting the mind in the physical reality of simply being here—the experience is *just this*. In a way, we can say that *just this* is the only answer to the koan-question "What is this?" This is not an intellectual or factual answer—it's the nonconceptual experience of the present moment. Moreover, the answer is constantly changing.

In working with "What is this?" the practice is not to focus on getting an answer, but to simply stay with the question. To stay with the question, with the visceral experience of the anxiety and confusion of not knowing, is where the question can eventually resolve itself. It resolves itself through the doing. The doing is sitting with the physicality of our present moment experience. In this case the present moment experience *is* the anxiety of not knowing and all of the sense of lack, depression, and loneliness that may be on board.

It may take many sessions of staying with this question, but as we truly reside in the physical experience, at some point it may be like popping a balloon, where the anxiety and confusion and the need to know just disappear. What remains? *Just Being.* And when this happens, the sense that life will never be enough is no longer an issue. The question of meaninglessness is no longer a question.

This is a key aspect of what the practice of meditation is about—staying with our present moment experience. We don't have to have an explanation for why meditation is good for us. We can say that sitting still in meditation helps settle the body and mind, but the fact is, until we sit and experience this for ourselves, no explanation will satisfy us. Yet, when we learn to sit in silence, just staying with our internal experience, we come to realize that it is the most real thing. To just be with our experience, even when it's difficult, can transform into the genuinely satisfying and meaningful experience of just Being.

The satisfaction we feel comes from the doing. The meaning comes from the activity. We can add on explanations after— that may help somewhat with our answer-seeking mind. But again, the real answer comes from the way we live. This is the answer to how we can experience meaning. *Meaning is possible in one place alone—which is here, in exactly what we are experiencing right now.*

Some have asked whether we can experience a meaningful life given the certainty that we will die. This question can even be reduced to nihilism—if we're going to die, why bother to seek meaning? Yet it is the very knowledge that life is temporary and that we don't have endless time that makes meaning possible. This is one of the essential gifts of aging.

The awareness that comes when we realize we don't have limitless time allows us to actually live in the immediacy of the present moment—including simple things like seeing, hearing, tasting food, appreciating little things about the people we're around. It also motivates us to prioritize doing what is most important to us, like deepening our relationships, being in nature, or pursuing activities we may have ignored for far too long, like writing, artistic pursuits, or volunteer work to better the planet in any number of ways—thereby furthering the possibility of experiencing our life as meaningful.

So, where do we find a sense of meaning when we no longer feel productive or have a solid identity? The answer is: instead of trying to establish a new identity, we can cultivate our inner life and a sense of presence. *Being present—truly present—feels inherently meaningful.* It is meaningful because we are committed to experiencing our life in whatever activity we're engaged in.

When we're not trying to get somewhere or become "somebody," it is more likely we can learn to be at home with ourselves. Genuine equanimity is the natural byproduct of experiencing life as inherently meaningful. It includes the understanding that life is constantly changing, that both good things and bad things will come our way, and that we have very little control over almost anything. Learning to surrender to this, no longer demanding that things go a particular way, allows us to simply be. This doesn't mean we don't care, nor is it defeatism—rather it is a conscious acceptance of life as it is.

Although we certainly all want to be happy, the real purpose of human life is to awaken to who we truly are. The more we are in touch with who we really are, the closer we are to living a meaningful life of genuine happiness. As we learn to reside in our present moment experience, we may gradually discover that our true nature of connectedness is always available to us. We're no longer just trying to survive, or seek pleasure, or make mental sense of things—all of which cut us off from the mystery of our Being. Interestingly, when we get a taste of our basic connectedness to life, we may discover our aspiration to give from the natural generosity of the heart—including our inherent capacity for kindness and appreciation. Although there is no one secret to living a genuinely happy life, the deepest happiness of equanimity grows with our ability to stay with our present moment reality. This is also where we can find the meaning that all of us are looking for.

Granted there will be times as we age that life will seem quite difficult, and a sense of meaning will elude us—and perhaps it may feel like the last thing we'll want to do is stay fully present with our difficulties. But we may discover that trying to turn away from our suffering, and even from thoughts of our death, just makes matters worse—as does indulging them by getting lost in them.

What I have learned from working with physical pain has taught me a middle ground. When things seemed at their worst, instead of giving up and wallowing in self-pity and despair, I found that the most difficult circumstances have led to a deepening of my understanding. I may not like my experience, but the fact remains that whatever is happening right now, regardless of how unpleasant it is, is simply what life is; it is part of the natural order of things.

We all have pain. We all suffer. And we all will die.

Whether or not the small mind *wants* those things is not the point. When we can understand and accept that this is the natural order of things, we can more easily take the next step and surrender into our experience, to be fully present to whatever it is. Sometimes all this takes is to simply ask the question, "What is this?"—and then breathe into exactly what we are experiencing in the present moment.

Surprisingly, we may find that this practice actually results in a lightening of our spirits—allowing us now to approach our situations, even the difficult ones, with a subtle sense of humor. It's not as if we now see life as a joke (that would be much too simplistic, and also unrealistic); it's more that we no longer take ourselves, and especially our thoughts, so seriously.

Being fully conscious that we don't have endless time, and consequently being willing to truly be present with the time we have left, can even lead to the experience of meaningfulness and joy.

10

Reflection on Death

RIGHT after my seventy-second birthday I wrote this short piece:

Daily Reflection on Death

I know I am going to die.
I don't know when or where or how,
yet it's an inescapable fact
that my life will someday surely end.
During the process, there may be physical pain,
emotional distress, or mental decline.
But however it unfolds, the fact remains:
everything that I am will no longer be;
everyone that I care about will no longer be;
all that I do will no longer be.
This, right now, will no longer be.
This is not a lament!
It is simply the natural order of things:
that the body gradually breaks down and eventually dies.
To deny this, or complain, or fight it—is to suffer.
To accept this, surrender to it, and embrace it—
is to be free.

My intention was to recite this four times each day—an intention I've kept to fairly religiously since then.

Prior to this I found it extremely difficult to actually take in, on a visceral level, the fact that I will surely die. Something seems to be almost hardwired in humans that makes truly facing our death very elusive. The illusion that we all subtly hold is that we have endless time. This leaves us convinced that our life will continue indefinitely into some vague future. We are rarely aware of the extent to which this belief keeps us skating on thin ice, oblivious to the very real fact that our lives can end or be drastically altered at any time, without any warning or preparation. It keeps us in the state of "waking sleep," cruising through life in a numbing automatic way, so that we don't have to experience the anxiety of facing the certainty that we will die.

This anxiety is certainly understandable. Our survival instinct is to continue to live, and while this instinct can help us when danger arises, it also stands in direct conflict with the fact of our mortality. This conflict tends to bring discomfort, and since our desire to avoid discomfort is very strong, we mostly put the fact of our death out of our minds, perhaps doing everything we can to avoid it through the endless pursuit of pleasure, diversion, and busyness. Even when we get a visceral inkling that we don't have forever, within a nanosecond the insight is replaced with thoughts about something we have to do, or the trip we have planned, or even something as mundane as what we want for dinner. All of this serves to affirm our aliveness, and keep awareness of death and impermanence out of consciousness.

It's true that some people think about death; some are even preoccupied in an almost neurotic obsession with it. They may interpret every new physical symptom as proof that they have cancer. Or, if a loved one is late getting home, they may quickly jump to the conclusion that they've been killed in a car accident.

But such ruminations are mostly just negative mental spinning, far from genuine existential awareness.

On an intellectual level, we know we're going to die—yet we don't *really* know it on a visceral or experiential level. So the truth of our inevitable death is rarely taken in, again, because we fear that it might lead to overwhelming anxiety. To help us avoid this anxiety, and to help us remain oblivious, we humans often adopt the unique and peculiar delusion that we are "special"—in the sense that death and the difficult challenges that can precede death don't apply to us. We would, of course, probably deny that we believe this. Yet, even while we might readily admit that we are all subject to the biological process that birth inevitably ends in death, on a day-to-day level, we nonetheless remain oblivious to our mortality.

I was a hospice volunteer for ten years, and in my many encounters with the patients who were expected to die within a short time, I only met one person who wasn't caught in some form of denial. Even though death was on the immediate horizon, most seemed to need to hold on to the unconscious belief that they still had plenty of time. The fact that we can maintain this stance even when death is looming is evidence of our mind's brilliant talent for avoidance. As T. S. Eliot said: "Humankind cannot bear very much reality."

Certain classic belief systems have evolved in most cultures to shield us from the anxiety, and sometimes even the panic, of actually confronting the fact that we will die. Whether we believe that we go to heaven, rejoin with God, or become part of some vast cosmic energy, the purpose of these belief systems is to give us the comfort that through our spiritual perpetuation we don't really die, and thus we can avoid confronting death as the end of "me."

Religious belief systems are certainly not the only way we

make ourselves feel somehow "special"—in the sense of being invulnerable. Some identify strongly with their race or country. This allows us to feel that we're part of something that will continue into the indefinite future. Others may find a similar comfort from identifying with a higher cause or even with a leader. Some find this comfort in having children who will carry on their legacy, or in the thought that they will live on in the hearts of those they have loved or helped, or in writing books or making art—anything that gives a sense of immortality to "me." Although these various comforts may give us a temporary respite, we can't deny that they can also be a subtle way of trying to avoid facing the facts, and our fears, around dying. Denial isn't the only motive for these things; however, to the extent that it is, we need to acknowledge it to live more honestly and authentically in our remaining years.

Despite the strong instinctual aversion to facing our own death, as well as the deeply embedded cultural protections, most of the wisdom traditions agree that we ultimately have to come to grips with the visceral understanding that we will, in fact, die. Many even emphasize the view that this understanding can be truly transformative. But for this to happen, we may have to experience some kind of life crisis—something to push us out of our complacency and challenge our illusions. It may take the death of someone close to us, or a serious illness, to bring us closer to an inner understanding that we will with certainty one day die, and that we can't avoid the fact that we are not special in this regard. When we are jolted out of our complacency by a life-altering crisis, we may feel lost and betrayed. It may be hard to see how this experience could possibly make our life better.

When I was in my late forties, I had an acute and lengthy flare-up of dermatomyositis—a serious immune system disease in which my muscles would attack themselves, leading to severe weakness, pain, and unrelenting nausea. Along with the physical symptoms I also had psychological symptoms of self-pity, anxiety, depression, and helplessness. Although I didn't consciously believe I was dying, there was still the fear of death and, perhaps more so, the fear of dying in pain. For the first few months, I have to admit that I wallowed in feeling sorry for myself, and could not even consider how my experience could be transformative. But gradually I came to understand that this difficulty could actually be a path to becoming free. In fact, when I started to recover, I became a hospice volunteer to help keep myself from falling back into complacency. I felt that by staying close to the edge—to the reality of death—I would be less likely to lose sight of what was most important. There's something about being with dying people that makes our normal oblivion to death hard to maintain, and because of that I continued as a hospice volunteer for ten years.

Another, even more difficult experience for me arose after I had surgery for kidney cancer. Because of complications from the surgery I had chronic and sometimes intense nerve pain that has since persisted. It was out of this experience that I realized the need to honestly examine my relationship to death. I was fortunate, because I still had the time and energy needed to process all the resistance and detours that arise when we begin to face our mortality. If we wait until we have a terminal diagnosis, it may be too late to begin the work of trying to live more authentically.

We don't have to make this mistake. At some point, living a life of complacency, busyness, and diversions may no longer be satisfying, and we may naturally begin to revisit our priorities. This can sometimes be painful—yet recognizing this may also give us the freedom to choose to live in a new way. Regardless of our age or state of health, making the effort to acknowledge our inevitable death is a good beginning. Just as a life crisis adds poignancy to our day-to-day experience, so does the change in perspective that comes with recognizing our mortality. What this will look like is very individual; for some it may mean making the effort to communicate more genuinely with those we care about the most. It could mean devoting more time to prayer or meditation, or whatever brings us closer to living in the present, with a greater appreciation for life. The realization that we don't want to put off living in accord with what is most important to us can help us be grateful for what we value most, rather than continuing to indulge the fears that keep us from living most genuinely.

As I've said, one of the things that has proved most valuable to me is seeing from a larger perspective, which has been made possible by reciting the "Reflection on Death" several times a day. In reciting this, I pause with each phrase or each line and try to take it in as I breathe a little more slowly than usual. The benefit of doing this only manifested gradually—yet from the beginning I had a deep sense that this was important for me to do.

In the beginning there were days when the thought of my actual death would trigger strong anxiety. Other days I would feel very little—almost numbness. And in honesty, there have even been a few days, when my physical pain was particularly bad, that the thought of my death was almost a relief. But repeating the verse day after day has begun to bring a sense of light and space around what at first felt dark and grim. Although it's possible when we first realize that our life will surely end to get caught in a pessimistic view of life, this isn't necessary. It's a detour. In fact, the opposite is true—I began to understand that life and death are a natural process, and acknowledging this repeatedly allowed this understanding to become more real on a visceral level, and at the same time less anxiety-provoking.

The first line, "I know I am going to die," is the essence of this reflection. It's an acknowledgment of an objective fact that we normally fail to consider. The truth that 99 percent of our planet's species have already died makes it difficult to ignore this fact of life or justify our denial. Death is inevitable; no one can avoid it or get around it. It doesn't matter how rich we are, or how smart or powerful or accomplished—to be born means that we will inevitably die.

The second line, "I don't know when or where or how," helps clarify and make more specific the comprehension of our mortality. If we have persisted in believing that we have end-less time, it's a sobering fact to consider that we could die next month, next week—or tomorrow. To really consider this is a wake-up call—as is reflecting on *where* we might die. Do we picture ourselves dying at home in our bed? Or in a hospital? Truly, we could easily die somewhere we would never consider.

Our reflection becomes even more specific when we consider *how* we might die. It's likely that most of us would like to imagine dying painlessly at home in our sleep. But this is certainly not a given. Perhaps we will die peacefully from old age, but there's also a good probability that we will die in discomfort from illness or disease. It may be difficult to even consider this, but the surprising thing is that by truly taking this to heart, we can free ourselves of the hidden fears that we don't normally want to face.

Once we reflect on when and where and how we might die, the next line, "Yet it's an inescapable fact that my life will someday surely end," puts an accent on the essential theme of this reflection. The word *inescapable,* for me, makes our impermanence a reality. Even though we already know this intellectually, it is no longer just a piece of mental knowledge; it is now a specific reality that applies to "me." We need to allow this reminder to penetrate to our very core.

The next line can be particularly difficult to consider: "During this process there may be physical pain, emotional distress, or mental decline." We may know that our bodies won't last, but when our bodily systems start to break down, and when our memory starts to go, it is difficult to avoid getting caught in emotional distress. It may start in our knees or feet or hands or back. For some it hits the eyes, and for others the digestion or circulation. No part is immune from breakdown.

Fear, self-pity, and depression are sure to arise as the body begins to decline. The main reason this can be so difficult to consider is that *we still somehow expect it to be otherwise*. We still see ourselves as "special"—in the sense that normal biological processes don't really apply to us. Yet, as we repeatedly reflect on the fact of impermanence—including the breakdown of our body and mind—we gradually begin to include ourselves in the natural process of birth and death. We may be humbled, but we no longer feel betrayed.

The next lines make the reflection very real: "However it unfolds, the fact remains: everything that I am, everyone that I care about, all that I do—will no longer be." This has been true for everyone who has ever lived or who is living now. When I say these lines, I'm basically feeling what it means to no longer be. I picture my various identities or roles—as husband, father, teacher, friend—and see that they will no longer be. The same is true of my cherished relationships.

Even though my loved ones may survive me (although they too will surely one day die), the relationships will disappear with my body, as will all the things I believe to be important—all the things I'm attached to: enjoying my time and activities with Elizabeth in innumerable ways, taking walks along the ocean, sitting quietly in meditation, reading, writing, teaching, cooking, playing Ping-Pong, and on and on. All of these will be gone. Realizing this is not for me an exercise in being morose; rather it wakes me up to the wonder of being alive *now*. I can see how easy it is to spend my days on autopilot—not truly appreciating the things I claim to value most. This awareness allows me to live my day differently: prioritizing the things I most value and remembering to feel gratitude for what I have, since I'm aware that one day they will all be gone.

To truly highlight this understanding, the next line, "*This*, right now, will no longer be," brings awareness into the immediacy of the present moment. Sitting in my chair, reflecting and feeling the meaning of this line, makes it crystal clear that this moment will never be repeated—that *right now* is all there is. This new awareness puts all of our petty and negative things in a new light: excessive worries about aches and pains, concerns about stocks going down or bills to pay, questions about whether some food will make us fatter or clog our arteries, anxieties over success or image, or other innumerable vanities. Although it's obvious how much these petty worries cause us to suffer, we still cling to them with a stubbornness that defies reason. Fortunately, reflecting on our death allows us to see these worries and concerns in a clearer perspective. The lines of a haiku by Basho make this point with crystal clarity:

> Summer grasses—
> all that remains
> of warriors' dreams.

The next line—"This is not a lament!"—is important to acknowledge. When we take in the reality of death, and especially when we picture the possibility of the physical and emotional distress that may come as we age, it is very easy to fall into nihilism or depression or hopelessness. But the point of this reflection is to relate to these same facts in a new way—not as something to lament. Thus, the next line: "It is simply the natural order of things: the body gradually breaks down and eventually dies."

Seeing our life (and death) with a clear perspective—as a natural process that all living beings will go through—allows us to relate to it with a degree of lightness and freedom. It also allows us to give up the sense of being entitled—the feeling that this shouldn't happen *to me*. This is not just a mental process or intellectual knowledge—reflecting in this way allows this truth to be taken in on the level of the heart. We can feel it and understand it as a living reality.

The next line describes how we may spend much of our time: "To deny this, or complain, or fight it—is to suffer." We certainly can see how long we have denied the reality of our death, how long we have maintained the illusion that we have limitless time. And yes, even though we may have enjoyed the ephemeral pleasure of skating on the thin ice, something inside of us knows that these illusions are indeed illusions. That is why we spend so much time struggling to fill our time—with busyness and diversions—as a way to avoid considering what is always right in front of us. Facing our fears will never be our first choice.

When the reality of our aging can no longer be denied and we experience the disappointment of failing bodies and declining minds, our natural inclination is to complain, catastrophize, or wallow in self-pity. But does it ever help to complain or indulge in self-pity? Doesn't it guarantee that we will suffer? The same is true as we try to fight each new piece of evidence that we are not immune to aging—trying to cover the wrinkles and sags and bulges or searching for exotic remedies for realities that are just part of how life unfolds. Even exercising can be a form of fighting against the inevitable. I'm not saying we shouldn't exercise or do whatever we can to keep the body healthy; it's only problematic when we have the mindset that our efforts will stop the inevitable decline.

Some people push themselves hard in an attempt to overcome whatever symptoms they may have. When we think of ourselves as strong, we may believe that we can override our perceived weaknesses. But this is just foolish, since it comes out of pride and the fear of being—or appearing—weak. At some point it has to become obvious that we can't remain healthy or youthful forever. Trying to get our old life back just leads to unhappiness, and the unhappiness continues and deepens as we try to fight the inevitable again and again. Isn't it true that we always suffer when we fight against things that we cannot change?

The last line of the reflection tells us exactly what we need to do: "To accept this, surrender to it, and embrace it—is to be free." This is not easily done, of course, but the effort does not need to be a grim struggle.

When we see our life and death as a natural process—that life is finite and that dying is to be expected—it becomes easier to take in more and more, and to see more and more in clear perspective. That is what it means to acknowledge it, as the first step in acceptance. It starts as conceptual knowledge and then, as it becomes more and more embodied, it deepens into an understanding grounded in the body and in the heart. This is a gradual process, which is why I recite the reflection several times each and every day. In this sense it is like a prayer, but the only thing we're asking for is true understanding.

Once we accept the reality of our mortality, the next stage is to surrender to it—to cease our resistance to what is. Unfortunately, we can't simply force ourselves to surrender; we can't just drop our resistance to experiencing the reality of our eventual death just because we want to. What we *can* do, however, is focus all of our attention on the exact state of our own mental, emotional, and physical experience, and then breathe into it, letting the breath provide space for it all. In other words, we *feel* the totality of our life in that moment, and rest in it, reside in it—letting it just be. This is not the surrender of resignation, in the sense of feeling defeated, but that of no longer resisting what is. As we breathe into our experience, as we sink into it, we go a little deeper with each in-breath.

There is one step after surrender: embracing our fate. The basic teaching is that we have to eventually learn how to embrace the anxiety over the certainty of our mortality. The great existentialists—from Kierkegaard to Nietzsche to Heidegger—all taught this. Kierkegaard cautioned that we can't skip confronting death head-on, for if we do, we would deny ourselves the possibility of ever experiencing transcendence. This means we may have to feel the dread and panic that accompanies facing our death, including feeling lost and helpless, but as we do this with increasing consciousness and intentionality, it is nonetheless the path to becoming inwardly free. When we sense the finality of no longer being here, and feel the chill and want to turn away, instead we open our arms to it and embrace it.

But how do we do this?

This requires a subtle shift in our attitude—to a mind that

can open to and say "Yes" to whatever is there, to a genuine wanting to go to the root of one's fears, to face such fears and feel them fully. This means bringing a full awareness to the thoughts, emotions, and bodily sensations that compose our anxiety. Sometimes, when I'm doing the reflection and I get to the line about embracing my experience, I realize how I've been caught in identifying with my fears or my pain. But on reading the line and saying Yes to my experience, occasionally my shorthand phrase "Do your worst" comes to mind—not in a grim or forceful way, but more as bringing a kind of lightheartedness to the situation.

In surrendering to our experience we are essentially no longer resisting, and instead we're letting our anxiety just be there. Embracing goes one step further, by *actively engaging* our anxiety—which is a very different thing from mere anxious worrying. It's good to remember, though, that some days embracing may not be possible. Some days we won't even be able to surrender. But most of the time we will be able to at least accept the reality that we don't have endless time. And when the little mind in anger asks, "Why me?" the clear-seeing mind understands that the answer is "Why *not* me?"

Nietzsche and Heidegger wrote extensively on the need to embrace death head-on in order to truly experience what life really is. They affirm the view that without a real awareness of our death, we are not really alive. Normally we identify with and indulge our fear-based thoughts and emotions, but as we embrace death's unavoidability, these thoughts and emotions, which normally seem so real and so solid, become more and more porous and insubstantial. Although the unfolding confrontation with the reality of death may sound grim, in actual fact, it is more grim to sleepwalk through life, missing out on the richness and depth of living from kindness, appreciation, and love—the qualities that emerge more readily when we live with honesty.

The basic underlying principle is this: *awareness heals*. To embrace the reality of our death means to willingly and consciously bring our full awareness to it. By facing death squarely, we paradoxically free ourselves of the anxiety that surrounds death and begin to learn to live more authentically. Even if our transcendence is not complete or permanent, we may still enjoy a degree of freedom from anxiety that we have never thought possible.

For me, reflecting on my death every day has been a process of turning away from complacency and turning toward what is most important. In this process I've been forced to look at myself with a penetrating honesty, which includes facing the fears that have held me back from living from my true heart. I've seen the choices I've avoided, the actions I've not taken. Feeling the remorse of an *unlived* life has resulted in a renewed look at my priorities and a wanting to connect with a deeper reality. In reflecting on how I want to spend my remaining time and energy, what I've discovered is that reminding myself every day that we are surely going to die can ultimately direct me toward clarity and love. As I make the conscious effort to go against my fears and my deeply conditioned patterns, something transforms in my being, and I can more naturally tap into the love and connectedness that are the nature of our Being.

In this sense "Reflection on Death" is not so much about dying as it is about learning how to live fully. For example, for some time Elizabeth and I have both experienced the phenomena of not being able to remember people's names or certain words. At first it was frustrating, even a little scary. We couldn't help but wonder if dementia was right around the corner. But accepting the gradual decline of the mind is part of understanding the natural course of a human life. Without this acceptance, the alternative is denial, self-pity, complaint, or futile struggle—all of which lead to suffering, and away from living with the peace of knowing our place within the natural order of things. Now Elizabeth and I often fill in words for each other, but instead of it being a source of worry, we usually just smile—this is just how it is!

Even though I've had many friends and relatives die in the last twenty years, and witnessed dozens of deaths as a hospice volunteer, these experiences did not have the same effect on me as doing the "Reflection on Death." More than anything, doing the "Reflection" has helped dispel the deeply embedded illusion that I have endless time. As a result of doing the "Reflection" there are definite changes in my priorities and life perspective, as well as subtle changes in how I am now living my life. There is more honesty in my relationships, less dwelling on petty worries, and less willingness to allow anger or fear to dictate my life. I definitely feel lighter, with more equanimity, am more appreciative, and am certainly less entitled. Probably most important, I am able to experience and express love more readily.

Throughout the "Reflection on Death" there is no mention of what death is or what might come after we die. The truth is: I don't know. In fact, I don't know if anybody really knows. But this shouldn't stop us from doing the essential work of looking at our own relationship to the fact that we will someday surely die. Reflecting on our death is another way of asking, "Do I want to stay stuck in complacency and fear, or do I want to follow the path of living from a more open heart?"

The more we become aware of the certainty of our mortality, the more we can use that awareness to appreciate the preciousness of the ephemeral nature of reality. This is expressed beautifully in one of my favorite Zen haikus:

> Life is but a dewdrop
> Trembling on a leaf—
> And yet ... and yet ...

Three Life-Affirming Exercises

The following exercises relating to your death might prove to be not only interesting but potentially transformative.

Your Timeline

Draw a horizontal line on a page representing the time from birth to death. Write the word *Birth* on the far left of the line and *Death* on the far right. Place a short vertical line where you imagine you are on this timeline.

First, reflect on what this means for a few moments—to feel the reality that you don't have endless time.

Next, given the amount of time you imagine you have left, write down any reprioritizing that you may think is called for.

When you're finished, reflect on what you want to do differently going forward.

Your Obituary

Write a short obituary—just five to six sentences—on your qualities as a person, as if they were written by someone who really knew you. Write it as if you died today.

When finished, consider if it provides any insight into yourself that might make a difference in how you live.

Your Tombstone

Write down what you would ideally like to have written about you on your tombstone—just one short sentence.

This one line represents your highest aspiration, and it is something that is worthwhile to consider every day.

11

Cultivating Connectedness

As we age, and particularly as we realize that we don't have limitless time, it becomes more and more important to focus on what is most real. We understand that we can't keep putting off the efforts to come to a genuine sense of the profundity of what life really is. Even if we've lived a good life, including maintaining a spiritual orientation, we may still be painfully aware that we have missed something that is essential. We may feel that there's an as yet unmet yearning to experience our true nature of connectedness and love, and know this *as a living experience.*

We can, of course, talk about the interconnectedness of all and everything, and certainly make intellectual sense of it. We can on some level understand that the air we inhale, that we call the breath, is the same air that is all around us—that there is truly no distinction between the inside and outside air. But to understand this connectedness conceptually is very different from an experiential, firsthand taste.

We may occasionally have a moment of grace and have an actual living sense of our basic connectedness. We may hear a bird sing, for example, and as the bird's song pervades us and fills us, the whole world seems to open up. And sometimes, at the end of a long meditation retreat, we may have a sense of the undividedness of things, or we may have the sense of well-being, or completeness, when life feels connected, even without putting words on it. This often comes as a result of making efforts to stay present for long periods, where we cultivate an intensified awareness. This intensified awareness allows us to become less caught up in believing our thoughts, and in believing that our thoughts, our emotions, and our bodies are the totality of who we are.

But the fact remains that, even after such moments of connectedness, we can return to the old habit of believing firmly that we are a single, permanent self. The power of our long-standing patterns means that the living truth of interconnectedness rarely moves beyond an intellectual understanding or a brief glimpse—even though observation can readily show us that the belief that we are a separate and permanent self is really just an illusion. We can observe in both ourselves and in others that we are really a collection of many personas, many selves we might call "me." Which "me" predominates depends on which self-image or identity we're holding on to at the moment.

One place we can see this is in the way the mood we're in determines how we see things: if we're in a bad mood, people may seem to be irritating, whereas if our mood becomes better, the exact same people may seem fine to us. A more telling example: how many times have we firmly pledged that we won't engage in a particular behavior again, such as drinking or overeating, only to soon find ourselves doing the exact thing we sincerely believed we wouldn't do? Given that we have examples of similar situations every day, how can we continue to believe that we are a single, unchanging self? Yet, this is exactly what we do.

Liberation involves waking up from the illusion that we're separate beings somehow cut off from others and the world. Seeing through the illusion of a separate self means recognizing that the "self" we're taking ourselves to be at the moment is incomplete, inaccurate, and at best only a small part of who we are. Seeing this with clarity is what helps us to transition from the sense of separation to experiencing the interconnectedness with all of life. This interconnectedness can be described in many ways. Whether we call it "God," or oneness, or the universal nature of things—what we're talking about, and can experience, is the unity that encompasses all of the forms in which reality appears.

It's important to understand that our firmly held views about how things are determine how we perceive and experience reality. And as long as we unconsciously assume that our notions of being an independent and separate self are true, we will continue to perceive and experience the world as disconnected. Even when we have occasional tastes of interconnectedness, our beliefs and assumptions of being an unchanging separate self still tend to override these experiences, and those tastes have little lasting impact on our conditioned views of being a "me."

What is needed, I believe, is an actual practice of connectedness, where we can regularly experience it as a visceral reality. Over time, after repeated experiences, our deeply seated assumptions of separateness may be challenged and become somewhat less solid. As our conventional view of reality as being a world broken up into many separate and unrelated parts is challenged, it is less likely to dictate how we perceive and experience the world. As a result, we may begin to experience reality increasingly as the unity that it is.

The experience of our basic connectedness is not necessarily the same as having a Big Flash of Total Oneness. Although that's certainly possible, what's being described here is more the slow breaking down of the barriers that the mind normally erects—a dissolution of the barriers between ourselves and almost everyone and everything.

It's good to keep in mind that every meditation practice or style has pitfalls. The pitfall of a meditation on cultivating connectedness is that we could easily fall into craving some special experience—of trying to feel a particular way, such as "feeling at one with everything." But if we simply follow the instructions, which include paying attention to whatever arises—including the desire to feel some special way—we can avoid the trap of being caught once again in the detours that keep us mired in our conditioned view of reality.

The following meditation is designed to cultivate the experience of connectedness. I've been doing this meditation regularly for the last few years, and although it's sometimes difficult for me to do—in that it requires both intense concentration and a stretching of the "awareness muscle" beyond its normal capacity—nonetheless, I have found it to be a very powerful practice.

One of the keys to doing this meditation is to bring attention to *the whole of oneself,* which is a unique bodily experience that is sometimes described as the feeling of "*I am here.*" With regard to this, however, please understand that when we experience "*I am here,*" it's not the little "I" of the ego experiencing it; it is from the larger sense of who we are. It is where we no longer identify with our thoughts or our feelings, or even our bodies, as all that we are.

But again, we're not *trying* to feel connectedness; rather we're setting up conditions where our natural connectedness can come alive.

One note: this is a somewhat sophisticated and difficult exercise. No one is expected to master it in a few sittings. It took me months of doing it daily to be able to actually experience it. More specifically, it takes a while to get past the technical instructions, which may at first seem very wordy and effortful.

Yet, with some practice it becomes more natural, and the effort is more of a soft intention to just be here.

I suggest you start by doing this meditation for just five to ten minutes near the end of your normal meditation time—just to get a feel for what's possible.

Yes, we have our unique self, *and* at the same time we're a part of a dynamic wholeness. As John Muir said, "When we try to pick out anything by itself, we find it hitched to everything else in the universe." So we start with the breath, and then include the body, and then expand into the environment—allowing us to open into the inextricable connectedness of all existence. In these moments, we identify with a vaster sense of what life is.

We may even have moments where we're acutely aware that we *are* the vastness, as well as a unique manifestation of it. As one famous Chinese Zen teacher once wrote: "I meet myself, which includes everything I meet." And this is where the word *connectedness* becomes more than just a word. This understanding embodies the deep wisdom that "all is one."

Here's the practice:

Meditation on Cultivating the Experience of Connectedness

When doing this practice, be sure to pause long enough to really feel each of the parts before moving on. To help avoid a dreamy subjective state, keep the eyes open.

Adjust your posture, so you are relaxed yet alert.

Now bring the attention to the breath.

First feel the breath as it goes in and out of the nose.

Feel the coolness on the in-breath and the subtle texture on the out-breath.

Stay with this awareness of the breath for three full breaths.

Now feel the breath in the area of the chest for three full breaths, breathing as if you were breathing directly into the center of the chest.

Feel the rising and falling of the chest area, and with each breath breathe a little more deeply into the chest center.

Now feel the breath in the area of the abdomen for three full breaths.

Feel the specific physical sensations in the belly on each inhalation and exhalation.

Now let awareness expand, so you can feel the full experience of breathing.

Simultaneously feel the breath in the nose, in the center of the chest, and in the belly.

It's okay to flicker between the three areas, to give the interconnectedness a chance to emerge.

Stay with this full experience of breathing for at least three full breaths, feeling it in the various areas of the body, letting the central focus move to the center of the chest.

Thoughts will arise in the mind. Just notice them, and put them on call waiting. Do the same with any judgments. Or any desires to achieve a special state of mind.

Keep coming back to the full experience of breathing—feeling the breath as a whole in the nose, the chest, and the belly.

Stay here for a few more breaths.

Now let awareness expand to include the whole body.

Start with bringing attention to the sensations of the head and the upper torso for three full breaths.

Next include the sensations of the arms and hands for three full breaths.

Next include the sensations of the legs and feet for three full breaths.

Feel the felt-sense of the whole of yourself, almost as if you were just outside of yourself, including the head and torso, the arms and hands, the legs and feet.

Feel the various parts spring to aliveness as you bring attention to them.

Feel the vibrant field of total bodily aliveness.

Feel your own presence.

Feel the body sitting there—the existential experience of "I am here."

You can even say the words "I am here" silently to yourself, to help tap into the experience.

Stay with this experience for at least three full breaths.

Now let awareness expand to include the environment.

First feel the air around you for three full breaths. Feel its touch on your skin.

Next, for three full breaths, hear the sounds—both near and far. Don't try to name the sounds, just be present with the auditory experience.

Next sense the feeling of space in the room for three full breaths.

Now stay with the total experience of the environment for three full breaths—feeling the air, hearing the sounds, sensing the space in the room.

To experience the basic connectedness of breath, body, and environment, now try to bring awareness to all three elements at once—moving attention gently back and forth from one aspect to another.

Feel the breath in the nose, the chest, and the belly, focusing on the center of the chest.

While staying with this, notice the felt-sense of the whole of oneself—the head and torso, the arms and hands, the legs and feet. Feel the whole of your presence.

While staying with the full experience of the breath and the felt-sense of the body, include awareness of the environment—the air temperature, the sounds, the sense of space in the room.

Moving quickly back and forth from the breath, to the body, to the environment, try to feel as much of it as you can at once.

Allow the various aspects of body and environment to be held in a single field of awareness.

Stay with this for several breaths.

Sense how everything intermingles in an interweaving tapestry of breath, body, and environment.

Silently say the words "I am here."

Slowly say each word for one full breath, repeating the whole phrase "I am here."

Sense your presence, your Being, simply sitting here.

With the eyes fully open, feel your connection with whatever else is in the room.

Feel your connection with the space outside of the room.

Come back to the breath, the whole of one's body, and the environment—no longer feeling isolated and separate.

Experience the connectedness that you are for a few more breaths—feeling the interweaving of awareness and energy.

Within the inner stillness and silence, feel the Love that is the nature of our very being.

To *know* the Love that is the nature of our Being, to truly experience this, is to be awake or "enlightened"—even if only momentarily. What is enlightenment other than gradually becoming free from our very limited bubble of perception? Normally we think we see reality, but what we see is our own subjective perceptions, filtered through our language and conditioning—which includes all of our associations and desires.

We create this protected world in order to survive and make sense of things, yet when we live only in our bubble of perception, our life narrows down to a solid world of fixed boundaries, cutting us off from the totality, the mystery of our Being. This is why this meditation cultivates awareness of physical reality, rather than just mental concepts—to help us gradually open into a wider and more spacious awareness. Starting with mindfulness of the breath, and then increasingly opening out of our limited sphere of awareness, we can begin to experience our basic connectedness. We can even perhaps have occasional tastes of the vastness. As the curtain of separation lifts, we begin to understand that we are more than just our thoughts or just our body. As this understanding gradually develops, we begin to experience, within ourselves, the connectedness that life truly is.

This brings us closer to fulfilling our life task: to know the truth of who we really are—that the nature of our Being is connectedness and love.

Tapping into our basic connectedness also allows us to understand what it truly means to say Yes to our life. This has to include saying Yes even to our difficulties and pain. We understand that the joy we have felt in our life is inseparable from the pain and the losses; all of these are inextricably connected. All of the pains, as well as our mistakes, our weaknesses, and our attachments, are a necessary part of our development. All of those things we have so disliked have nonetheless pushed us in our growth and are necessary parts of the totality of where we stand in the present moment. We are, in effect, saying Yes to all of it, embracing all of it. This is the direct path to becoming who we truly are.

It will often take courage to say Yes to our difficulties and our losses, rather than succumbing to self-pity and fear. Over the course of our life journey we may forget this many times and find ourselves going off course—but it's not necessary (or helpful!) to judge ourselves for each wayward detour. Again, each detour, each backslide, is part of the path of learning and growth, and if we are to affirm our life, to say Yes to it, we must say Yes to *all* of it, detours and all. Experiencing our basic connectedness means we're acknowledging the whole of what our life is and being willing to truly live it, just as it is.

Returning to the words of the Buddha: he exhorted us to remember that we are not here forever, and that we should remind ourselves that each day could be our last. The truth is, we have no idea how long we have. We never know what will happen next. We don't even know what's right around the corner. But if we remember that we have limited time, we can begin to understand that each day is precious, and that we should never take anyone or anything for granted. We can stop wasting so much of our life replaying the past, worrying about the future, or staying stuck in complacency. As a longtime hospice volunteer, I can't even the count the number of times I witnessed patients dying with regret.

Through practices such as the ones in this book, we can begin, perhaps for the first time, to take our life seriously, and move more and more in the direction of cultivating the experience of connectedness and love. I certainly experience this in my relationship to nature—being able to increasingly see and feel the plants and trees, and especially the ocean, which is right outside my door, as not separate from me. We can begin to truly appreciate the people around us—and the fact that they, too, have limited time.

Since I have been doing this meditation on cultivating the experience of connectedness, I have found a much deeper satisfaction in teaching meditation. Now, when I work with individual students, even though I may have more learning and experience than they do, I don't feel like I am any different from them, and it is so much easier to feel the connectedness rather than the separateness. This is even more true in my shared life with Elizabeth. We can still differ on any number of things, of course, but what now defines our relationship, more than anything, is the love we share: the wanting to extend ourselves and "do for" one another.

For all of us, in all of our relationships, why would we want to continue our self-centered and small-minded behaviors toward others when any one of us could die at any time? We certainly wouldn't want someone to die while we were angry at them or filled with petty thoughts and judgments about them. All we need to do is look into another's eyes and remember: Everyone has pain. Everyone suffers. Everyone will die. Love is what remains when we can experience another as they truly are, without judgment.

When we are able to cultivate the experience of connectedness, we can tap into one aspect of what is considered the deepest wisdom: that "all is one." As we take this understanding into the heart, particularly as we can feel into the suffering that all of us share, we can tap into the other aspect of deepest wisdom: that "all is love." Again, returning to the words often purported to be from the Buddha: "In the end this is what matters most: How well did you love?"

12

Renewal

WE'RE ALL BEGINNERS when it comes to aging. And, although the fact that we are in new territory can certainly contribute to the difficulties in dealing with getting older, it can also have a very positive side. Aging can be seen as a new phase of our life: a phase of renewal. Nowhere is this more evident than in our opportunity to devote more time to reflection and inner exploration. The result, regardless of whatever physical limitations we may be experiencing, is the possibility of cultivating and living increasingly from kindness and gratitude—two of the essential qualities of a life of satisfaction and equanimity.

Kindness

Kindness, especially toward ourselves, is often not so easy to access. It seems that most human beings have the ingrained belief that on some basic or fundamental level, they're not okay. Most people feel or fear to some extent that they may not measure up, or that they are "less than" others. How this comes about is another topic, but the fact is, when we look honestly within ourselves, we're likely to see that there's a fundamental self-doubt on board, even if that belief stays unconscious most of the time. This is why the ability to extend kindness to ourselves, exactly as we are, is so essential.

In addition, how we feel about ourselves is often determined by external validations, like how we look, how others regard us, and for many, by our success. If these are the things that make us feel worthy, we may not yet understand that basing our own worth on such external factors is like building a foundation on sand. As we get older, appearance and "success" may be on the decline, and if we're fortunate, we'll begin to understand that a true sense of worth does not come from externals—but rather from knowing who we are and our place in the world. This too can be cultivated through the practice of kindness toward oneself, where we learn to accept ourselves exactly as we are in this moment.

The problem is, when things seem to go wrong, including having the body's capacities begin to decline, we're very well trained at getting down on ourselves, as if we're somehow failures. We see ourselves as not enough, and this kind of self-judgment leaves us feeling isolated. We forget that we're simply human, and that nobody's life turns out according to our hopes and dreams. Bringing kindness to ourselves allows us to see our common humanity—that everyone has pain, and that everyone struggles at times. Bringing kindness to ourselves, in specific ways, allows us to drop our self-judgment and experience our own worth—a worth that is not based on external appearances or so-called success.

When we can cultivate this kind of understanding, we no longer have the same fear of "failure." Watching our plans about "how it's supposed to go" be derailed, we start to understand more deeply that it's simply human to have setbacks, and seeing this gives us the inner confidence to persevere. This is why, as we age, or at any point in our lifetime when we're experiencing illness or difficulties around getting older, being able to extend kindness toward ourselves when we're feeling distress is no small thing.

Kindness is a precious commodity. Think about this: can you remember a time when you wished for some kindness, some empathy, and there wasn't any? On the other hand, can you remember a time when you were scared or felt isolated and were perhaps unexpectedly greeted with kindness, and what a gift that was?

In my case, some time ago I saw a doctor who was head of the pain clinic at a large university. I told him about the nerve pain I'd been experiencing for the last few years, and when I was finished describing my symptoms, he basically said, "You have a difficult condition, and truthfully I don't think there's anything that will really help." I was somewhat shocked by his words, but also by his manner: there didn't seem to be any empathy at all. And when I left, I had the passing thought that I didn't ever want to see another doctor again. But two days later I had an appointment with the head of another pain clinic. I described the same symptoms, and he basically said, "This may be difficult to treat, but there are a couple of things that I think might help, so let's give it a shot." It wasn't just his words, but also his presence and his kindness that felt healing.

You may wonder how you can cultivate kindness, both toward yourself and toward others. One tried-and-true method is through regularly doing a kindness meditation. Basically it teaches us to refrain from judging ourselves and others, and allows us to stop being critical of every real or imagined flaw. The essence of kindness practice is to actively extend unconditional friendliness, as the natural expression of the generosity of the heart. It's about cultivating an attitude of mind in which we wish for the welfare of everyone. With kindness, we experience a sense of connectedness, of innate goodwill, perhaps accompanied by a sense of openness that diminishes the mind's tendency to constantly judge.

Here is the basic kindness meditation that I do daily:

Basic Kindness Meditation

Either sitting or lying down, take a couple of deep breaths, relaxing into the body.

Become aware of the breath and begin to follow it into the center of the chest.

Whatever you feel, just be aware of that.

With each in-breath let awareness go a little deeper.

To activate the quality of kindness, first think of someone for whom you have very positive feelings. Picture them as clearly as you can. Breathe them in.

Let your innate kindness be activated by these positive feelings.

If there is no sense of warmth or kindness present, simply notice this, and continue.

TO ONESELF:

Staying with each line for a few breaths, say to yourself:

> Breathing in, dwelling in the heart.
> Breathing out, extending kindness to myself,
> exactly as I am right now

Relate with a benign friendliness to whatever you're feeling. You're basically wishing yourself well.

Breathing in, dwelling in the heart.
Breathing out, attending to whatever blocks kindness
and love.

Notice wherever you are caught in self-judgment or anger
or closed-heartedness—and let awareness heal.

Breathing in, dwelling in the heart.
Breathing out, extending kindness to others.

Feel the generosity of heart in extending kindness to others.

Repeat the above lines one more time.

TO OTHERS:

Now think of someone close to you, to whom you wish to
extend kindness.

Breathe the person's image into the center of the chest on
the in-breath.

On the out-breath extend kindness to this person while
repeating the following lines, staying with each line for a few
rounds of the breath.

Breathing [this person's name] in,
dwelling in the heart.
Breathing out, extending kindness to [name],
exactly as you are right now.

Wish for them a benign friendliness toward whatever they're
experiencing right now.

Breathing [name] in, dwelling in the heart.
Breathing out, may you be healed in your difficulties.

Basically wish for them that they learn from, and perhaps become free of, their difficulties.

Breathing [name] in, dwelling in the heart.
Breathing out, may you extend kindness to others.

Wish for them the ability to feel for the well-being of everyone.

You can repeat these lines to as many others as you wish. Start with people for whom you have positive feelings; later you can experiment with trying to extend kindness to those with whom you may be having difficulties, but it is better not to push this. We may need to first work with our own anger and resentments before it's possible to extend kindness to others. (I'll talk more about this shortly.)

Initially there may be some discomfort in doing the kindness meditation, including a lot of internal resistance. However, no matter what you experience—whether it is awkwardness, resistance, skepticism or anything else—it is well worth it to keep practicing the meditation, and to do it daily if at all possible. As we do the kindness meditation on a regular basis, it is no longer just a meditation exercise; it becomes more a part of our renewal, where kindness increasingly becomes our natural response to ourselves, others, and life.

As a side benefit, because the kindness meditation requires concentration, it may generate a degree of calmness, which is often a byproduct of doing a concentration meditation. Also, as you breathe into the center of the chest, it may trigger the parasympathetic response in the central nervous system, which may add to the experience of calm.

And yet, to fully engage aging as renewal, we have to take a look at our long-standing attitudes and behaviors—the ones that may block our natural kindness from coming forth. One of the greatest impediments to extending kindness to others is our anger. I have heard it said that people mellow with age—and no doubt some people do—but I know for a fact that many don't. As a hospice volunteer for many years I observed that often patients seemed willing to hold on to their anger and resentment right up until their last breath. But for aging to be a period of renewal, it is crucial that we learn how our anger can be transformed into kindness.

When we take offense at others, we think our anger is the result of what they did or didn't do. This means that we use *their* behavior to justify *our* anger. But in doing this, we miss an essential point: that when we get caught in blame and justification, which fuels our anger and resentment, we have gone off track. As the Indian elder Black Elk put it: "It is in the darkness in their own eyes that people lose their way."

Anger arises, in part, by "choosing" on some level to live as a victim, insisting on being right, and elevating ourselves by putting someone else down. When we do this, we have cut ourselves off from the heart—from the love and connection that is our true nature. Instead, we have to acknowledge that it is our *own* darkness that has pulled us off the path, not the darkness of others. Even though others may have done something unskillful or unkind, which may at some point need to be addressed, this *never* justifies our unkindness or our holding on to our anger in return. This may be hard to accept, but *true kindness toward others can never be dependent on how others treat us.*

When we believe we are treated unkindly, or when we make demands of another that aren't met, it often leads to difficulties with intimacy or trust, to fears of criticism or rejection, or to feeling unappreciated or controlled. Most of the time we're caught up in believing our own expectations of how another should be. We expect people to appreciate us, save us, or at least not criticize us, and this guarantees that we'll repeatedly experience disappointment. This thwarts our aspiration to live from kindness. The alternative is to recognize that such difficulties are a mirror, allowing us to look within ourselves at what blocks our own heart.

Practicing with our anger requires becoming present to all of this, as a bodily feeling, without indulging our angry thoughts. Ultimately, this allows us to see that when people treat us unkindly, it is *their* action, born of *their* suffering, and often has little to do with us. We may still feel the urge to use their actions to justify our negative reaction, yet we should be aware that we have another choice: we can instead choose to turn away from blaming. Doing so gives us the opportunity to look at and process our own anger, hurt, and fear. This, in turn, allows us the possibility of relating to the other person in a new way. We are now able to see them in their all-too-human garb, as just another human being in pain.

Perhaps we may even understand that they were not trying to hurt us, but simply acting out of their own pain-induced closed-heartedness. This understanding is the essence of forgiveness, an essential part of renewal.

Another way of coming to this understanding is to say to ourselves, "Just like me." When we find ourselves judging another person's traits or actions, if we say, "Just like me," and then reflect on our own similar traits and actions (even if ours are in a very different-looking category), we will often see that we're really not so different from the other person, except perhaps by degree. Seeing this helps undercut the power of our judgments. It opens us to seeing our own painful tendencies, and how they are not essentially different from the painful tendencies of others. This helps us develop compassion, as we become aware of not just our own suffering, but also the suffering of others. Julius Lester's insight puts this in clear perspective: "History is not just facts and events. History is also a pain in the heart, and we repeat history until we are able to make another's pain in the heart our own."

In the phase of renewal, we increasingly feel empathy for the suffering of others as we gradually understand that we are all interconnected. From this understanding there is a natural urge to extend well wishes to others who are in pain. Moreover, when we practice kindness ourselves, we're at least intending to add a little bit of kindness to the universe. In this small way, we can help benefit the entire world.

The more we cultivate and practice kindness, the more our actions in the world come naturally from the heart. And when situations arise where we don't know what to do or say, we can ask ourselves the pivotal question: "What would it mean, in this very moment, to live from kindness and love?" As we breathe into the center of the chest, we allow the response to come not from the mind but from the heart. It is at this point that we may connect with the love that is our true nature, and be more likely to function as a channel through which love can naturally flow. Perhaps we can begin to experience the satisfaction of connecting with the kindness that is our true nature, and then learn to live from it as best we can, as a natural response to whatever life presents.

Truthfully, there are really no big secrets on the spiritual path—but if you remember nothing else, let it be this: with whatever arises, whether we like it or not, the main thing we can do is experience and work with *whatever* our life is, as it is, right now.

In waking up to the path of kindness, we no longer push away aspects of ourselves or others that we normally judge as unwanted or bad. Kindness, in part, requires bringing gentle attention to the very things that seem to block our way to it, including our own judgments and disappointment. We don't have to change our thoughts or feelings; we just have to be aware of them, be present to them. Only through awareness of them is it possible to refrain from acting on our unskillful tendencies. Making this a living reality may take some time, but awareness is what heals; this is one of the most fundamental tenets on the path of self-renewal.

Gratitude

Whenever I reflect on what I consider to be most important, the answer I keep returning to is learning to live from the kindness and gratitude of the awakening heart.

Unfortunately, it seems that if we truly wish to awaken the heart, we often have to first experience adversity. We may have to lose things we cherish, or feel our secure future dissolving right in front of us. This is why the process of aging, where adversity and loss are so commonplace, affords us the continuing opportunity for renewal.

Regardless of our past attitudes and habits that have kept us from the path of self-renewal, it's what we do with the time we have left that matters. Living a life that is inherently worthwhile comes from being present to whatever arises. This will require no longer clinging to our protections, our pretenses, our grievances, our complacency, or our small-mindedness. Over time, practicing such presence fosters the experience of gratitude for the actual value of every experience, including those we would normally not think to be grateful for. When we react to an experience with awareness and gratitude, even our most difficult circumstances can be transformed into nourishment for our Being. We may even notice, over time, that being able to experience gratitude also simply feels better.

It may seem strange to suggest that we could be grateful for getting older, especially given the culturally accepted view that aging is not something we are supposed to look forward to. It's a given that the body gradually tends to break down, we have less strength and stamina, and our memory may decline. But is the common cultural view that aging is something that we should dread the only way to see this? The fact is, if we wish to be fully alive, growing older is really the only option. And given the number of things that can go wrong with our bodies—the number is probably in the thousands—it's not a big jump to feel grateful for all of the parts of our bodies and mind that continue to work and allow us to appreciate the time we have left. Of course, there may be days when the aches and pains and losses outweigh the ability to feel gratitude, but in between the hard spells we can learn to really appreciate whatever quality of life we can still enjoy.

Gratitude can include reflecting on the people with whom we've shared enjoyable experiences. Even more so, it can include those who have helped us along the way. When we reflect on the people and experiences that have been important to us, we may want to call or write those we haven't been in contact with, but with whom we'd like to connect before it's too late. If a person is no longer alive, you can still speak to them in your heart.

I had a philosophy teacher in college who significantly altered the course of my life. He hardly knew me and I'm sure he wasn't aware of the very positive impact he had on me, but forty years after I graduated from college I decided to write him to thank him. I didn't know where he was or even if he was still alive, but I finally found him and wrote him a very heartfelt letter. To my surprise he wrote a letter in return, and to my delight, he actually signed it, "Love." "Love" was the last word I would have expected from him, as he was very private and emotionally unexpressive as a teacher. It meant a great deal to me, and since then I have felt the natural urge to express my gratitude to others much more freely.

In our reflections, along with remembering the things we are grateful for, we can also consider the regrets we may feel for things we have left undone, or may have done that have hurt others. Just as we might want to call or write people to whom we want to express our gratitude, we may also want to call or write to extend any apologies that we feel we might want to make. We need to do whatever we can to bring us closer to our deepest values and how we wish to live.

Another way we can enhance what is most positive in ourselves is by using the phrase "Just like me," which we used earlier as a way to help us drop our judgments of others. When we see someone we admire and recognize an admirable trait, if we can remember to say, "Just like me," we might be able to see that we too have that same trait, although perhaps not yet fully developed. Often we're blind to, or don't want to recognize, our own positive qualities, and part of extending kindness and gratitude toward ourselves is learning to see and appreciate ourselves without our habitual negative filters.

Knowing we don't have endless time allows our appreciation and gratitude to go deeper in a more natural way. One of my favorite quotes, from the artist Paul Klee, paints a very poignant picture of the depths to which our appreciation can go: "Imagine you are dead. After many years of exile you are permitted to cast a single glance earthward. You see a lamppost and an old dog lifting his leg against it. You are so moved that you cannot stop sobbing."

Every night, I try to do the following nightly meditation on gratitude before I go to sleep. My recommendation is to begin this meditation before you get too mentally or physically exhausted, and try to do it at the same time each night.

Nightly Gratitude Meditation

Begin in a relaxed posture, perhaps lying on your back, with hands folded on the center of the chest. Eyes can be open or closed.

Make an effort to recall the main events of the day, starting with the first memory of the morning, taking care to not to get pulled into thinking, analyzing, associating, or judging.

This is a simple review, an observation in hindsight. Recall, as objectively as possible, the facts of what actually transpired.

Stay grounded in your physical presence by keeping awareness on the breath in the area of the center of the chest. Without this grounding, the reflection can easily become too mental. If you get caught up in mental activity, return to this grounding.

Ask yourself: "What am I most grateful for today?"

Find at least three things from the day, large or small, for which you feel genuine appreciation, even though you might not have felt gratitude at the time.

For each of them, think to yourself: "I am grateful for that."

Take a moment to reflect that there is much to be grateful for.

You may wish to create a "gratitude journal," a notebook in which you record each day the three things for which you are grateful. Doing this may bring a little more precision and discipline to the reflection.

By doing the nightly reflection regularly, we not only become more grateful during the meditation itself, but it also spills over into the next day, as we become more aware and receptive to noticing gratitude in real time. We begin to notice that as we go through our daily routine, little positive moments are often not even acknowledged—but as we become more attuned to what is actually happening during the day, these moments begin to stand out, and gratitude is more likely to become a regular response in our daily living. We may even want to silently say, with each moment of appreciation, "I am grateful for this."

In reflecting on gratitude, it's helpful to consider these light-hearted yet interesting words from a Buddhist teacher: "Let us rise up and be thankful, for if we didn't learn a lot today, at least we learned a little, and if we didn't learn a little, at least we didn't get sick, and if we got sick, at least we didn't die. So, let us all be thankful."

CULTIVATING KINDNESS AND GRATITUDE are crucial if we wish for our remaining years to become a period of renewal. This renewal is not something that will happen overnight; no doubt there will be days when we need to be shaken out of our complacency and be reminded that most of the things that concern us are of little importance—how we look, our insecurities, our mundane worries. The more we can truly understand that we don't have endless time, the more we can connect with what really matters to us—which allows us to prioritize more clearly how we really want to spend our time and energy. Even when things are difficult, by staying attuned to our priorities we can connect with a quiet joy that makes life feel worthwhile.

It has not been easy for me to break through my own dense filter of denial—the assumption that my life would continue into the indefinite future. Some days I clearly comprehend the fact that my life will surely end—and then the old habitual filter may fall back in place, and I have no awareness of how or when that happened. But for me, one of the benefits of aging is that it is so full of reminders that my time is limited that it now is increasingly difficult to pretend otherwise.

Truly, this is exactly how I want it, since it allows me to keep my priorities in clear view. Each day, I prioritize spending plenty of time in meditation and in reflection. Each day, I try to never take people for granted. And each day I practice cultivating kindness and living it the best I can. As well, I cultivate gratitude daily, literally acknowledging my blessings, both big and small.

Keeping these priorities in clear view also helps me give myself more freely and honestly in relating with others, helping me recognize the inherent human value in everyone, and not getting caught up in things that don't ultimately matter. Living my priorities allows me to dedicate myself to my life task of learning to say "Yes" to everything, to experience the connectedness that we are, and to live increasingly from the love that is our most authentic way of being.

Priorities may be somewhat different for each of us. For some, deeper communication with loved ones may top the list; for others, a willingness to take risks or to refrain from being captured by our fears. For some, simply living in the present as fully as possible may be what's most important. For all of us, living more from kindness, gratitude, and love will hopefully make the list.

And yet, no matter how clearly we see our priorities, there

will be cloudy days, and sometimes dark nights, when nothing seems clear. This doesn't mean we've failed or that we're on the wrong track. What it means is that we're still beginners in this process of aging. I have had to learn this over and over again.

And like all beginners, we often will have to start again at square one. Yet there can be comfort in understanding the wisdom that there are no Big Answers that are going to explain the mystery of life or take away our pain or our dark nights. For me, it's enough to know that this sometimes wonderful, sometimes difficult journey is really not so complicated. We are born, we live, and then we die—this is the natural order of things. And everything in between—including all of our struggles and difficulties—is also part of the natural order of things. Everyone has pain. Everyone suffers. And everyone will die. When we don't understand this, we take all of the in-between things much too seriously. My wish for everyone is this: to truly take seriously just one thing, which is the commitment to living, as best we can, from kindness and love.

About the Authors

Ezra Bayda and Elizabeth Hamilton have each been practicing meditation for over forty years and teaching since 1995, including leading retreats in the United States and abroad. They currently co-teach at Zen Center San Diego.

Ezra is the author of seven books, including *Being Zen, The Authentic Life,* and *Saying Yes to Life (Even the Hard Parts)*. Elizabeth is the author of *Untrain Your Parrot* and has led numerous workshops at hospices.

What to Read Next
from Wisdom Publications

BEARING THE UNBEARABLE
Love, Loss, and the Heartbreaking Path of Grief
Joanne Cacciatore
Foreword by Jeffrey Rubin

"Simultaneously heartwrenching and uplifting. Cacciatore offers practical guidance on coping with profound and life-changing grief. This book is destined to be a classic . . . [it] is simply the best book I have ever read on the process of grief."
—Ira Israel, *Huffington Post*

SAYING YES TO LIFE
(Even the Hard Parts)
Ezra Bayda with Josh Bartok
Foreword by Thomas Moore

"Astonishing."—*Spirituality & Health*

About Wisdom Publications

Wisdom Publications is the leading publisher of classic and contemporary Buddhist books and practical works on mindfulness. To learn more about us or to explore our other books, please visit our website at wisdomexperience.org or contact us at the address below.

Wisdom Publications
199 Elm Street
Somerville, MA 02144 USA

We are a 501(c)(3) organization, and donations in support of our mission are tax deductible.

Wisdom Publications is affiliated with the Foundation for the Preservation of the Mahayana Tradition (FPMT).